D1628822

FUNEN

The Heart of Denmark

Cover: Egeskov Castle, the Knights' Hall.

Overleaf: Aerial view of Egeskov Castle.

DENMARK IN PRINT & PICTURES

FUNEN
The Heart of Denmark

AN ACCOUNT

WRITTEN BY A GROUP

OF ITS

INHABITANTS

DET DANSKE SELSKAB

The Danish Institute for Information about Denmark
and Cultural Cooperation with other Nations
Kultorvet 2, DK-1175 Copenhagen K.

1980

Translation:
Graham D. Caie
Ann Caie

Printing:
AiO Tryk as, Odense

Reproductions:
OR 2, Odense

ISBN 87-7429-032-0

Printed in Denmark

Contents

The Island Region of Funen

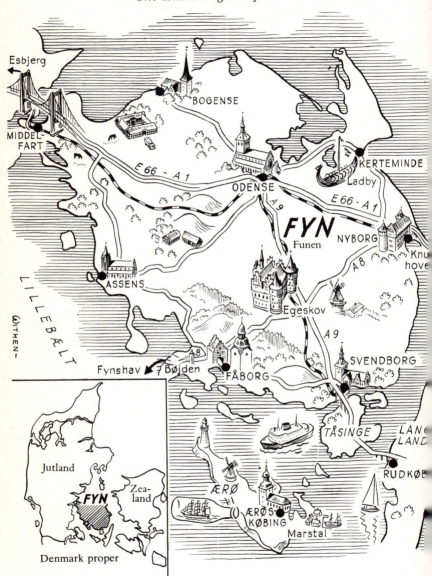

Esbjerg

MIDDEL-
FART

BOGENSE

E 66 - A 1

KERTEMINDE

ODENSE

Ladby

A 9

FYN
Funen

E 66 - A 1

NYBORG

Knu
hove

ASSENS

A 8

LILLEBÆLT

Egeskov

WITHEN-

A 9

Fynshav

Bøjden

A 8

FÅBORG

SVENDBORG

TÅSINGE

LAN
LAND

RUDKØB

Jutland

FYN

Zea-
land

ÆRØ

ÆRØS-
KØBING

Marstal

Denmark proper

Foreword

The intention of publishing a book about Funen, written for foreign readers by the people of Funen themselves, *Funen – the Heart of Denmark,* has been considered for some time, but it appears in print now just at the right time.

The development in Europe on the threshold of the 80s is influenced, as it happens, by a new movement, regionalism, which, allied with the classical European tradition of diversity in unity, wishes to give prominence to provincial areas, cultivate and promote the distinctive values and traditions of the local area.

This is exactly what we aim to do in this book on Funen, Denmark's heart. Encircled by sea and straits, Funen has preserved its unmistakable distinctive characteristics, even though it is the corridor between Zealand with the capital and the so-called "mainland" of Jutland. At the same time Funen has, in keeping with the best in Danish tradition, "receptiveness for the unknown and adherence to our own"; to a marked extent this means a union of its specific regional character with aptitudes and contributions on a universal scale. This is the case to an equal extent with art, knowledge and business life.

As will be seen in this book some of the greatest names in Danish cultural life, art, knowledge and business life are connected with Funen: Hans Christian Andersen, Carl Nielsen, H. C. Ørsted, Rasmus Kr. Rask, C. F. Tietgen. It was also on Funen that the Danish Folk High School and Free School seriously took root and flourished, spreading to the rest of Denmark.

Hans Christian Andersen was particularly influenced by receptiveness for the unknown and adherence to our own.

As a boy he left, as is known, his at that time small place of birth, Odense, and went to Copenhagen in order, as he himself expressed it, first to experience such a terrible lot and later to be famous. The remarkable happened, namely he gained European fame with his fairy tales and stories before he was really acknowledged in the capital city; this was due not least to the fact that he continued to reflect in his work the Funen and Odense of his childhood, the world of the provinces with its grandeur in small things, ordinary people, life and reality included in the wonderful world of fantasy and dream of the fairy tale.

The composer Carl Nielsen retained the same links with his childhood world on Funen; his music, from his popular songs and the Funen choral work to his great symphonies, is inspired by the popular rhythm and nature of Funen.

The school of painting called "Fynboerne" with Johannes Larsen and Fritz Syberg to the fore, followed by a large group of painters, reflects the essence of the region of Funen in their numerous compositions.

Funen with its many industries also reflects the fact that culture and business life are two sides of the same coin. Numerous active enterprises, some of which are among the largest in Denmark, provide a solid basis for Funen as a society that is influenced by humanity and productivity.

In my dual capacity as mayor of Odense municipality and chairman of the Funen branch of the Danish Institute it is a special personal pleasure for me to introduce Funen – the Heart of Denmark with these words and to thank the authors and translators.

Verner Dalskov

Funen – the Heart of Denmark

by Peter Eriksen

Funen is no longer at the centre of the world, as many of its inhabitants believed in days gone by, but it is still at the centre of one of Europe's smallest countries. It is called the heart or the garden of Denmark or "the butter lump in the porridge", as the beloved child has many names. It is both the busy motorway corridor that connects Europe and the North and yet it is hidden in its own, private calm. Only the native of Funen can travel inside the boundaries of the kingdom right around his island and, to his great joy, only meet fellow countrymen! Hans Christian Andersen frequently mentions the island of his birth in his fairy stories: cottages, ditches and the manor dam, windmills, streams, the green mantle of the beech woods that cling around the coast. But his country can be situated anywhere, just as his characters are not especially natives of Funen.

Not one Danish poet in the history of literature has really had the courage and powers to describe the countryside of Funen, perhaps because Funen itself is a poem and its beauty exceeds the poet's imagination. The island has a distinct face, but it is difficult to become familiar with its fine net of smile-wrinkles, as it is so luxuriant in its sweetness, love of order and intimate idyll, that tourists from harsher zones sometimes catch themselves wondering if it is indeed not too beautiful to be true? And they have every justification to do so, for Funen is the result not only of nature's but also to a large extent of man's diligent efforts. Some might call it an arrogant attempt to poach on our Lord's creation.

Funen consists of a group of 25 inhabited and many more uninhabited islands, which cover an area of 3,482 square kms and has almost half a million inhabitants. In spite of its small area this part of the kingdom occupies a central position not only on the map of Denmark, but also in the history, politics and cultural life of the country, thanks to a people who are more shrewd and cooperative than their neighbours on either side of the water that surrounds the island. In spite of the fact that Funen has attached itself on to the region of Jutland to the west by as many as two bridges, while it expects to be connected to Zealand to the east over the Storebælt by what will be the continent's largest bridge, the local inhabitants know their role, just as those who reconcile opposite opinions, smooth out differences and, in addition, when it is a question of art, new school reforms, industrial and social experiments, also act as bridge builders.

The native of Funen is born on Denmark's best soil. Even so it was sparsely populated when the first peasants in ancient times battled with stone and sand in other areas. It was simply too good. The oldest plough could not manage the heavy and rich topsoil, the primitive stone axes were not able to hack a path through the woods, which at that time grew like green fortresses around the villages, which were simply small clearings in the vegetation. Just as poets feel themselves superfluous, so also the first cultivators when they met all this luxurious fertility were forced to acknowledge that there was here more than *they* had the power and ability to conquer.

And what was even more remarkable – in a country that for thousands of years was the gateway of Scandinavia, where races marched, thrusting forward and retreating, Funen lay hove-to in the middle of storms raging from its borders. The peninsula of Jutland was ravished and laid waste, as happened to Zealand with Copenhagen and the lands in Skåne in Sweden which belonged to the Danish crown, while the narrow straits placed their gentle, protective hands around Funen. For that reason the dark events that occurred in the past are remembered here more than

The willow with its squat body and long, struggling branches is the national tree of Funen.

in other parts of Denmark. If one were to believe the local accounts, the Swedish wars of the 1660s were concerned with Funen alone. The damaging effects are still remembered and the achievements of the Danes of hundreds of years ago are also remembered with fervour. On Funen the tragedies are strongly and vividly felt and have not faded by the matter-of-fact records found in history books.

Could this be connected with the impressionable, sensitive and musical temperament of the native of Funen and his strong sense of catching the prevailing mood? Denmark, that little land, has space for a greater degree of contrasts, as far as national characteristics are concerned, than foreigners think. You will not find here any of the brooding Prince Hamlet of Denmark of Shakespeare's drama. The native of Funen is a remarkable mixture of innocent cheerfulness, gregarious hospitality, conscientious application and greatly conscious of his homeland. He adapts his need of play and competition to both work and play. Although Funen is made a dense and closed land by the many hedges, the native of Funen himself is accommodating and open. But intimacy is found only in a closed circle and within every circle is another, even more closed. The native of Funen has still new rings in which to ensconce himself, rings which are the freemasonry of tact and are built on a culture which is strongly founded in the home from which he never ostensibly cut himself off.

Even during plague, oppression, wars and famine in the Middle Ages and later times the peasant never forgot to plant willow and brushwood between the fields, grafting and hop growing. He did all in his power to erase all traces of need. Farms, gardens and hedges arose out of the indefatigable desire of the native of Funen to protect the position of home, to find an outlet for his creative abilities and as a protest against malicious damage and destruction, to fight for the right of beauty to develop. Mankind's right to be creative no matter what the circumstances.

The swift streams of the countryside that noisily babble on their way and take odd digressions, criss-crossing fields and woods, are closely related in their impulsive and spontaneous reactions to the many country roads of Funen. They take motorists by the hand and play a confused game of hide and seek with them between hills and in small copses, only to leave them finally – in the middle of a private farm. They do this in spite of tourism's demand that a road must have an official duty – or, in the language of Funen, impress the country that wherever we intend to go, the home is all-important.

The map boasts such names as Siberia, Pennsylvania, and the Funen Alps with their associations of famous places around the globe. But, placed in relation to the love on Funen of the immediate and easy-to-grasp everyday life which we ourselves create and influence, this is only a clever way of emphasizing the fact that the ocean is in the drop and the drop is in the ocean.

Once Funen was criss-crossed, as no other part of the country, with a network of private railways whose deserted station buildings and closed permanent ways are still to be seen as a sign of the fact that if one wishes to make one's world larger one must travel slowly and take up less room in it.

If a man from Zealand in Denmark is confronted with a heavy stone, he lets it lie there; the man from Jutland will split it, but the man from Funen will display it as a decoration in beautiful caves, as a sign post, watering trough, fence between fields or just to sit on and enjoy a beautiful view by the side of his thatched, half-timbered house. Around the island the old outdoor village meeting places are still cherished; here the inhabitants met to decide on petty and important affairs. This was the last place that they went out of fashion, but although political decisions are made in the elected municipal authorities, the old stones on which the masters of the guilds sat are still replaced and renewed.

The stone circle tells us much about the people who live here. It is hardly by chance that it was here that the country's first folk high school was founded in 1851 with 15 pupils in a small farm in the town of Ryslinge. The high school would scarcely have developed into the educational form as we know it in Danish culture without the skill of the native of Funen to create a circle of friends around it. Whereas in other places in Denmark the high school is an enclave in the region, it found here on Funen fertile soil in the combination of the practical yet beautiful, and the historical yet poetical.

Domestic industry, wood carving work, choirs, musicians and neatly kept gardens and houses on Funen reflect an intimacy amongst the people. The compact nature of the home demands that something fiery, undulating and closely-packed must grow around the farms of Funen. The inhabitants of Funen are not only famous for painting, they are also great frame-makers in hedges and fences. They never tire in their love of repairing, re-organising and embellishing. The countryside is protected by vegetation so that the wind loses its destructive force and wanders mildly and carefully in over the plentiful gardens that abound in fruit trees and vegetables, as beauty with its sensuous appetite for life must be felt, smelt, tasted by the people of Funen. There are indeed hills in the meadows but they do not dominate the scenery, which is open and spacious, but hills and valleys do not dominate. A ridge is entwined and held in by hedges and brushwood fences in order to conceal the pronounced lines and gaps – which thousands of swallows bind together in graceful loops. The garden of the native of Funen, the landscape around his home and the entire landscape is one large garden. In this way the circle is complete.

There are crofters' farm buildings with four wings built round a courtyard too small to turn a waggon in. But they are not built for any social ambitions, that is, like a manor house in miniature, for such an idea lies far from the way of thinking here. "One must only be vain in one's home and in front of one's wife", goes the old saying. So no one need boast outwardly. As a farmer's wife from Funen once said about her son-in-law with a deep sigh: "He is a hard-working and good-natured man in every way, but he has only one fault – he doesn't really bring cheer into the home".

The native of Funen's desire to conquer is subdued into a quiet, hankering initiative. The phrase "little Denmark" is not for him an expression of inferiority complex, but a mentality. When he speaks of a good little country, he thinks of – his own. But he believes that everything that is not tended withers and wastes away.

The language of Funen is like a short-handled whip with a long lash that sweetly sings when swung in the air – but woe betide any who are hit by the whiplash, as it certainly will be sore. But it takes a lot to provoke such an attack.

"He's a big chap, but he doesn't like to be beaten", the smith said about his neighbour, the innkeeper who was

"Yes, it ought to be fine, but it's rotten, and for how long can it go on?" A desire to strike a balance and a sense of proportion characterizes the people of Funen.

strong but cowardly. In spite of all the moderation in this statement, this is a hard judgement – on Funen.

The musical and high tone of the language on Funen is perfectly pitched – for women's voices. They love their native language on Funen: they say "moders mål" (mother tongue) deliberately in two words – and mean it literally. The girls on Funen are well known for their motto "The night is our own", which is not only aimed at the amorous nature of the night, but also shows a characteristic of the need to get their own way. Their slightly bowed back comes from their humble gracefulness which is in sharp contrast to their confident, self-assured behaviour. The dialect of Funen can, when heard by Danes from other parts of the country, conjure up the impression of being superficial and gossipy. Consequently it is often this dialect that is chosen to raise a smile in reviews and variety shows. But the native of Funen keeps his self-irony intact and can laugh along with the others, proud of his native land and of the fact that he can spread happiness, even in this connection. His wit is never hostile nor sly – at the most his wit will have an intentionally teasing undertone, aimed at bringing other folk down to earth. A farmer told his neighbour that he was going to slaughter something:

"I'll turn up tomorrow to give you a hand", came the helpful offer. "That's fine. You'll get the head, legs and blood". "No, no, that's far too much". "Not at all; of course it's only – a hen!"

Funen is a land of manors. But whereas in other parts of Denmark there is hidden scepticism for the aristocracy and the castle, for which the peasants worked like slaves in the old days, the native of Funen, without getting romantic or stylish, feels proud to look at them and show them off. But the feeling of size is connected with the sense of things of human proportions, the defenceless and the patient: solidarity between the strong and the weak, as is displayed in the intimate circle of the home.

A farmer's wife who had a chance to travel with her husband to a place where they could acquire a farm in freehold, convinced him to remain, since nobility for them meant the farmers' attachment to the land and villeinage to the manor farms. For, as she expressed it, "What can we do, other than put the ground to use? No one owns anything any longer – than to his death".

The inquisitive nature of the native of Funen can be measured by the friendly and smiling farmer who pops up in the village behind a heavily laden wheelbarrow and sets out, full of expectation, to meet the stranger. "If it's a neighbour you're going to visit" – he is trying to invent a message to him, to find out his real reason – "Ah well, he's gone to the market town half an hour ago; he's got to see to some payments at the post-office and as his sister is ill, he'll surely visit her after that and therefore not be home before late afternoon". Isolation and alienation betray themselves, disguised as a desire to help the wayfarer. There is indeed a fellow feeling involved, but he who is outside it, must be content with being informed of the fact, even if this is done hospitably.

The native of Funen is never bored. Tax on weeds and thistles, rather than tobacco and alcohol. But of course wild plants must have their place among the fauna of Funen – for the sake of disorder. So they appear, then, along the ditches and road sides where the red mouth of the poppy passionately kisses the pure, blue harebell. For it is a lyrical picture that fits in with the character of Funen.

The small and large islands in the Archipelago of South Funen constitute one of the country's most incredible worlds. Seafaring and agriculture. Farmers at sea and skippers' houses drowned in flowers. There are 72 islands that are uninhabited and which represent mankind's eternal desire in a pure way to rule a deserted island and establish a new and better civilization – their own – as the first and only inhabitant. But many of them are only small, grassy islets, often low and flat; the beach is stony or sandy and always bleached by much sun. The grass is squirted with white under a cloud of watchful birds. It usually pays to let the islands remain an unobtainable goal for our dreams as it is lost when gained.

Funen has given birth to the greatest number of Vikings in the Northern Regions in this mild country with sheltered waters. When English write about Vikings and Americans film them, it is always the Norwegian fjords which provide the romantic and dramatic background. But it was in the coves and fjords of South Funen that they learned to splash around, find out about wet and dry, always in the shelter and always on the look-out. In this maritime playpen the wild Norsemen emerged and here the foundations were established in the previous centuries for a large fleet with many wharfs for wooden vessels that carried the names of the small fishing villages of Funen all around the world.

This epoch is preserved in a number of small local museums which are the result of the personal efforts of enterprising idealists who are full of initiative. Will they and others be able to survive in their present form as publicly supported institutions? One of them is the museum in the market town of Fåborg, dedicated to the school of painting which in Danish art is called "Fynboerne" (the natives of Funen): "the peasant painters" they were contemptuously called by their contemporaries. But in fact they were anything but that. They were pioneers and men of the world gathered around one of the unaffiliated schools of art which grew up in Copenhagen in the 1880s, as a rebellion against the stiff, classical teaching of the Royal Academy of Art. They were brilliant artists, widely different in form and message but common in that they centred on the family life that blossomed in and around the home in Funen, which was just about all their world. It was here they were born and grew up. In their hands the working, amorous, playing man, surrounded by nature, gained a place in Danish painting. In the vestibule of the museum the Funen sculptor Kai Nielsen has erected a man-size statue of its founder and patron, the industrialist Mads Rasmussen. A true resemblance of a great man, but expressed in the manner of Funen – without hero's halo and with a subtle smile.

Odense, the region's largest and the country's third largest city, stands like a spider in the island's gilded web and sucks through a net of roads the power out of the small coastal towns, which garnish its edges. This at least is what the sceptics maintain.

But in their small streets is a stubborn will to live and sound resignation, and one good thing came out of it: thanks to Odense that attracts much of the progress to its centre, nature will not in the year 2000 be placed in a museum as a curiosity in a glass show-case. For it is a part of the handicraft of the island and therefore protected against malicious damage and disfiguration.

The many churches on Funen are a witness to the fact that in the market towns and villages it was the church that

w of the Svendborg Sound as seen from Svendborg, one of the most beautifully situated ns in Denmark.

The new Little Belt Bridge, opened in 1970, connects the island of Funen with Jutland. It is ‹ of the more than 30 bridges crossing Denmark's sounds and belts.

Svendborg is Funen's second largest town with time-honoured trade and shipping tradition‹

neral view of the Little Belt.

An artist's impression of a Funen landscape:
Above: Gerda Andrea Heltoft (born 1929): A Hill-crest. Overcast. 1976. (32×40 cm. Ow⌐
by Else Jensen).
Below: Niels Hyhn (1902–1950): Landscape Scene at Kærum. 1938. (70×90 cm. Owned
Simon Larsen).

annes Larsen (1867–1961): Mother and Child. 1899. This endearing picture of a mother
st-feeding her child, although small in size, expresses deep emotion.
annes Larsen, a very versatile artist, is considered one of the leading painters in the "Fyn-
-" school, the group of painters from Funen who lived and worked there. (50×41 cm. Owned
lse Larsen).
er painters in this group, whose works predominantly are to be found in Faaborg Museum,
Fritz Syberg (see plate 7) and Peter Hansen (see plate 9).

Christian Pedersen-Bellinge (born 1897): An August Day. 1977. The threatening storm is sensed by the dramatic sky. (80×90 cm. Owned by Bent Banke).

Thorkild Knudsen (born 1912): An Interior. Faaborg Museum. 1976. A classical study in perspective from the museum, which creates the setting for the artistic world of Funen. In the foreground is a sculpture by the famous Funen sculptor Kai Nielsen. (120×140 cm. Owned by the artist).

an Madsen (1898–1970): By Aasum Church. 1928–30. The light of an April day is
red in this triangular composition in which the white church rises up as the radiant central
. (95×121 cm. Owned by Herman Madsen and Charlotte Henriksen's Bequest).

Syberg (1862–1939): The Garden in Winter. 1925–32. The old trees' gnarled trunks and
pattern of branches creates a contrast to the straight lines of the farm house and the white
ing of snow over the garden. (Privately owned).

Edvard Weie (1879–1943): A Rubberplant. 1920. The nature of colour was a popular s▮
for discussion among painters in the beginning of the century. For Weie colour was primar▮
expression of sense perception and experience. This composition is a good example ▮
treatment of colour. (*Fyns Kunstmuseum*).
Though Edvard Weie is not a Funen painter, many of his works are to be found in the Fun▮
Gallery in Odense.

was the "town's hall" in ancient times, more than the townhall. The walls of the church were painted with scenes of the devil being defeated and a town fire averted. Important men when deceased had their sword and spurs hung up, while captains hung models of their ships. The church is a witness to a profound connection between it, and the town, which has now been lost nationally, but continues to exist in the home.

The willow tree with its stocky body and long, distended boughs like a mane is the national tree of Funen. But it is grown because there must be some magic and sorcery at least visually in this otherwise so carefree island.

The sprouting corn's green shoots on the chubby cheeks of the fields of Funen; the fishing villages, in which a man in colloquial speech is called after his boat, like a round generous hand that is caressed by fjords and the thin, cool fingers of coves; the low houses in the narrow streets of the market towns with inhabitants who, sitting behind window mirrors, both follow society's development in their newspapers and also the local inhabitants' activities outside their window at the same time! It is altogether a toy world taken right out of a fairy tale, but bubbling with vitality, because it wishes to be so; influenced by a people who do not believe in a fertile union in a new and outward-looking Europe, unless it is based on a specific character or identity.

Funen is swarming with societies for choirs, shooting, gymnastics and folk dance. The joie-de-vivre must be transformed into activity and developed – not only in work. People don't talk disdainfully of art, on the island which is itself a work of art, with the wind that sings, the birds that give concerts in their thousands in the treetops and the landscape that is one large and happy riot of colours.

The light can, because of the great difference in temperature between the ridges, woods, lakes and surrounding sea, suddenly transform itself into a camera, the lenses of which focus on the distant and veil that which is near. On such days there are soft and subtle over- and undertones.

There are both drama and magic in the light on Funen that can set its beautiful coulisses into motion. On the island's islets and isthmuses there are small samples of other Danish forms of landscape, just as harsh and weather-beaten. Here the legends and myths arise, as everywhere else where there is a projection from the sea, but they don't release fear. The keynote of those who have taken over Funen is one of sadness. Sadness that lies very close to the light and happy disposition. The sadness can be read on a gravestone on Funen, the text of which is written by the deceased himself. In it he pities greatly those who are still alive, who soon shall join him. Naturally it is in verse. For the musical native of Funen uses verse and rhythm when he shall pronounce his heart's innermost feelings.

Sadness because the Paradise on Earth inevitably is replaced by death's darkness. The Paradise on Funen — of course.

The Market Towns of Funen

by Henning Nielsen

"Odense, Bogense, Middelfart and Assens; Fåborg, Svendborg, Nyborg, Kerteminde". This is what Danish schoolchildren used to sing, when they had to learn the names of the Danish towns by rote – in this case the market towns of Funen. Nowadays we have also to include the market towns on the islands south of Funen amongst those in the administrative region of Funen: Rudkøbing on Langeland and Marstal and Ærøskøbing on Ærø.

It is not known if it were purely for melodious reasons that Odense was mentioned first in the school jingle, but in all circumstances there is something symbolic about placing it first, as there can be no doubt at all that Odense, which for long periods in Denmark's history was the largest town in the provinces, has always been the island's undisputed economic and cultural centre.

Odense differs from the other market towns on Funen by not lying directly by the sea. Moreover, Odense is Funen's oldest market town. Presumably this township existed long before it is first mentioned in 988 as an episcopal residence. It is situated on a low ridge north of Odense river, Funen's largest waterway, and only a few kilometres from the river's estuary in Odense Fjord. Large ships had therefore to berth at the village of Stige or at Kerteminde; it was only after the excavation of a canal from the head of the fjord into the town was completed in the beginning of the 19th century, that the construction of Odense harbour was made possible. The harbour has been expanded many times since then, just as the canal has been made deeper.

That was one of the conditions for the great increase in population which this market town experienced during the

19th century in connection with industrialisation and the flow of people from country to town, an increase in population which has continued through this century with an increase in, amongst other things, services and trade.

This drastic growth in Odense, while the development in the majority of the market towns on Funen stagnated, naturally led to the fact that the old town burst its boundaries and new built-up areas were established. The expansion of Odense presents a special case, compared with other Danish industrial towns, as it took the form to a large extent of individual houses, especially south of the river, and so a large part of the city came to resemble a garden city, which is still preserved.

In this century the growth of the city has followed along the highways that connect Odense with the coastal market towns; thus many of the villages in the area were transformed into suburbs, which in 1970 were connected at an administrative level to the old market town of Odense with the creation of the Greater Odense Municipality in connection with the municipality reform, which also meant for the other market towns on Funen the annexation of the nearby hinterland into the market town.

The most important exception to the prevalent tendency to form a garden city is the new part of the town, Vollsmose, east of the city centre, which is dominated by flats. In this way the tendency which is already found in single house areas is continued: namely to segregate into neighbourhoods often on social or prestige criteria, an outlook that is also found to a greater or lesser extent in the other market towns on Funen.

The rapid growth of the city meant also an increase in traffic and thus the penetration of roads (well known in many market towns) that deprived the town of many valuable houses which were well worth conservation. This occurred before the value of conservation work was realized in most places in the last decade, work that can prevent future demolition of houses which deserve preservation and which contribute to the distinctive character and special milieu of the city.

In Odense a road that leads traffic from the harbour and the northern part of the town towards the south has meant that the old part of the city was split in two. The district east of this boasts the best preserved old market town houses, while the network of medieval streets can still be detected during a walk round this district. Around the Hans Christian Andersen Museum, also, there is to be found an excellent example of the fact that restoration work can ensure the preservation of a district's distinctive characteristics, while providing modern home facilities. The district will also accommodate a congress centre.

Odense, as the capital of Funen, is naturally also influenced by the many institutions and industrial plants. Today most of these plants are moved outside the city. The town's centre, where one previously both lived and worked, had its residential use lessened in favour of offices, shops and traffic, while both homes and jobs in industry have been moved out to the periphery. This tendency is also seen in the other towns on Funen where suburbs and satellite towns, on the contrary, have grown rapidly in proportion to the spread of the car and especially after the creation of standard-built houses in the 1960s.

The smallest market town on Funen, *Bogense,* was the dominant one of North Funen in the Middle Ages with its major trade in corn and cattle; Bogense is, for instance, one example among many of how the market towns along the coast stagnated while Odense and Svendborg, the central town of South Funen, grew in size. Until well into the 19th century Bogense was practically a "paved village", the expression used by the National-Liberal politician Orla Lehmann for the many, small Danish market towns.

Many people have, in addition, maintained that the coastal market towns on Funen were in fact too close together for all of them to prosper and develop; but, as most enjoyed privileges that dated back to the 1200s and 1300s, none were interested in giving up their status as market town, even though they themselves languished economically for long periods, often more like a mixture of village and fishing hamlet than a market town, distinguished by its trade and business.

As far as Bogense was concerned the town hoped for an economic development after the establishment of the railway in 1882, but here, as in so many other places, it was instead the larger town – Odense – that conquered the surrounding area. In recent years Bogense has aimed at tourism to a growing degree by, for example, building a marina. This has been the more natural thing to do, as Bogense, because of the previously mentioned lack of economic development, has better preserved its old characteristics as a market town and is one of the few places where one can sense a little of the life of market towns in previous times. In particular the terraced houses in Adelgade display an incredibly well-preserved total effect, just as the symmetrical square – the highest point of the town – is encircled by low, uniform cottages from the beginning of the 19th century.

Middelfart has benefitted in its development as a market town by its situation as a natural ferry station to Jutland, but in that respect, however, was for some time overshadowed by Assens which, before 1864 when Denmark lost Schleswig-Holstein, was an equally central ferry station to these two provinces as Middelfart. The construction of the transverse railroad over Funen in 1865 naturally placed the final station in nearby Strib, but the railway meant in any case increased economic development and attracted public institutions to Middelfart. In addition the town had from ancient times a fishing fleet belonging to the Porpoise Guild, whose guild hall is the main attraction of the town museum.

The building of a bridge in 1935 over the Lillebælt that connected Funen with Jutland also meant increased attraction to the town which, like the other market towns on

Funen, has excellent examples of old market town architecture, best preserved in the area around the church.

As mentioned above, *Assens* was until 1864 the major export harbour to Schleswig-Holstein of, amongst other things, bullocks, and when this function suddenly was taken away from the town, it led naturally to a degree of stagnation which also continued after the re-opening of the ferry connection in 1921. The construction of a sugar refinery in 1885 and the concurrent introduction of a railway connection to Odense via Tommerup did provide a counterbalance to the stagnation, but all in all Assens had to share the same fate as other small market towns on Funen, that had to watch while Odense took the lion's share of the increase in the cities that industrialisation brought about.

As a result of this, amongst other things, the town centre in Assens is characterized by the old town plan with square, church and the almost square blocks that surround it, while the housing area, as in other towns, has spread outside the old town centre.

South Funen's smallest market town, *Fåborg,* was one of the first towns in the country which was aware of the value in preserving its old buildings and had a conservation plan officially registered which would ensure the perfect, old image of the town, primarily Holkegade and the houses just inside Vesterport, a unique medieval town gate, which attracts many tourists to the town today.

Many merchants' houses are preserved from the town's golden era with the corn trade of the 19th century when there was a large fleet of ships; these houses can give you an idea of this town's oldest function – the procurement of agricultural products from the nearby catchment area via the merchants and the reselling of wares to the hinterland.

Svendborg grew up in the lea of its protected natural harbour at the narrowest part of Svendborg Sound and enjoyed the advantages of a fertile hinterland which made it South Funen's largest town at an early date, with connections also to the islands of Tåsinge, Langeland and Ærø.

The prosperity can be seen in the examples of merchants' houses preserved.

Even though part of the old buildings, as in Odense, have been torn down in favour of roads and the expansion of business life, there are still preserved many beautiful examples both of merchants' houses and housing for trades folk and the occupational groups connected with the sea.

The rapid increase in population in the last 150 years has led to an expansion in the buildings on the hilly ground in and around the old town. The construction of the railway from Svendborg to Odense in 1876, to Nyborg in 1897 and Fåborg in 1916 increased the growth of Svendborg to the detriment of the small market towns on Funen and this development is even more emphasized after the construction of the bridge connecting Tåsinge to Langeland.

The reason for the establishment of the East Funen market town *Nyborg* was its important position as a ferry station to Zealand, which early in the Middle Ages led to the construction of a fortified castle which throughout the Middle Ages provided the setting for many important encounters in the history of Denmark. The small passage leading up to the south face of Vor Frue (Our Lady's) Church still has a medieval look, for example with Denmark's oldest vicarage dated at around 1400. Otherwise the town is characterized by the pure lines of many provincial houses in the simple style of the architecture of Neoclassical and Empire design built after the great fire of 1797.

The town plan in the inner part is still characterized by the fact that it was a fortified town until 1869, by which time the town had already begun to expand outside the ramparts, of which a small part are preserved.

Kerteminde was for ages the natural harbour with road connections between the peninsula Hindsholm and the more southerly part of Funen. The original part of the town is that which lies north of the narrow sound that connects Kerteminde Fjord with the Storebælt. The reason for Kerteminde's existence was partly its function as a trading centre for Odense – which ceased after the construction of the Odense Canal – and partly the extensive fishery, so extensive that it used to be said, "Everyone in Kerteminde is a fisherman except the mayor, and he spears eels". A great speciality was the fat flounders which were called "Kerteminde's aldermen"; this once gave the Danish King Frederik IV a fright when he heard during a visit to the town that the mayor had just dispatched two aldermen that day.

The image of the town is distinguished by the houses designed in neoclassical architecture of the 1700s and 1800s and the attractive overall effect is one of the reasons for another major industry in present-day Kerteminde, namely tourism. This is emphasized even more by the nearby summerhouse area.

Langeland's main town *Rudkøbing* has been restricted throughout history by the fact that the farmers on the island from ancient times have had the right to export their products and buy wares from abroad, and by the fact that Lohals and Spodsbjerg for a long time functioned as illegal harbours. Only in the 19th century was there any advance in the economic development of the town, but not so much as to prevent the town preserving its old appearance, for example, a row of half-timbered houses right along the main road Brogade-Torvet-Østergade. The bridge connection which came in 1966 did not alter the fact that Rudkøbing, like the majority of smaller market towns on Funen, has been in the shadow, as far as economic development is concerned, of the two magnets, Odense and Svendborg.

In 1864 Ærø was administratively joined to Funen for the first time and one can still notice an influence from Schleswig in *Ærøskøbing,* which until the middle of the 1800s was the major market town on the island with profitable business with Southern Jutland. In 1864 this foundation was undermined and stagnation was an inevitable consequence. Today the town is on the American tourists' top-five-list of places in Europe which simply must be visited and this is due to the unusually well preserved buildings. Not without good reason Ærøskøbing has been called a genuine set-piece for a Holberg play*, where one can see the projecting gables, the outside stairs and picturesque signs which have been removed in the other market towns of Funen in the name of development. The oldest house in Søndergade is from the 1600s, while the majority of the other houses date from 1730–1800.

Ærø's largest market town today is *Marstal,* which in the 1860s experienced an enormous boom with a lively overseas traffic. By the end of the 19th century Marstal owned more ships than Copenhagen, and the three-masted Marstal schooner sailed overseas to both America and Asia. The town's shipping received a blow when 42 ships were lost in the First World War, and later with competition from Svendborg; today pleasure boats largely dominate the harbour. But it is still clearly evident that Marstal is a shipping town. All roads point to the harbour, the most important part of the town and even the interior of the church is influenced by shipping. Most significantly the altar portrays Christ calming the storm on the lake and in the churchyard one can read this inscription on a grave:

Here lies Christen Hansen
At anchor with his wife.
He will not hove to before
He comes to God's throne.

Yes, Marstal is the skippers' town from among the market towns of Funen.

Of all the market towns on Funen only Odense can be compared in age with the villages which will be discussed in the next chapter. The circle of market towns around the

* Ludvig Holberg (1684–1754), comedy writer, called "The Danish Molière".

26

coast is younger, but they nearly all have their origins in the early Middle Ages when they were awarded by the king those privileges which are fundamental for the existence of market towns.

The privilege established that only market towns were legal harbours, that is to say, that only the merchants of that town could handle merchandise to and from the country population in the catchment area. Now and then in the charters the neighbouring hinterland is defined as a kind of "protection zone" in which only the town's merchants could purchase wares.

The connecting link between land and town was therefore the merchant into whose courtyard the farmers came with their wares and concurrently with an increasing prosperity, bought both necessities and luxury goods in the merchant's shop. Such a visit to the merchant was naturally a great event and the popular author of Funen, Morten Korch, has written the following about the merchant's function:

> To be a successful merchant requires a considerable knowledge of mankind and great tact. Empty flattering was good for nothing; friendliness, true understanding and especially good humour are required. It ought to be fun and festive to visit the merchant's house. The customers should enjoy coming there and return home with lively and happy impressions.
> A merchant should know his customers, not only the men, but also both wives and children and preferably their circumstances and trade.

Even though one can still see fine, old merchants' houses in the market towns of Funen, this original function is not preserved. On the other hand another of the market town's functions is still alive and experiencing growth just now, namely market trade. Trade in the market was also a monopoly of the market town which usually took place on a certain day in the week on which the farmers and market gardeners of the district offered their wares for sale.

The market towns still serve today as the middle man for

27

products and service functions for those in the neighbouring hinterland, who in many cases also have their place of work in the market towns. In recent years the shopping centres have been placed in the towns' immediate environs, while the cities' inner areas have tried to increase their attractiveness. For example, many market towns on Funen have created permanent pedestrian streets and in the summer their number is increased. Now shopping centres are constructed which are built on the old trading traditions of the market town, e.g., the construction of *Vintapperstræde* (Tapster street) in connection with the pedestrian precinct in Odense in 1977, which also in the name itself draws on the old trade and crafts' traditions.

One function of the market town, which is also continued today, is shipping. The harbour is both a place of work and a place where one can breathe freely in the town, like allotment gardens and parks. Many of the ports on Funen have traditional harbour celebrations every summer in which the town's summer guests can also participate.

A characteristic group of the population in the market town in addition to the merchants was the craftsmen who were organised into guilds, whose function included the regulation of the recruitment into the trade and to look after social obligations, but they were largely stopped at the introduction of freetrade in 1857.

The inhabitants of the market town directed the town's affairs by themselves from ancient times (only the market towns on Ærø did not have this selv-government before 1864) and only after the Municipal reform of 1970 were the market towns and country municipalities made alike with respect to municipal government.

Whereas 2/3 of the population on Funen today live in towns or in urban dwellings, 150 years ago there was only 15% and, as can be seen above, this population development occurred to the advantage of the larger market towns, especially Odense. Many of the smaller ones have more or less become stagnant and this situation is being studied now in connection with the preparation of a regional plan which should ensure a spreading of development to include the smaller market towns and country communities as well. The tendency to spread out has already begun; the place of work and the home are often far apart and, for example, Odense has relinquished many of its citizens to the housing estates in the surrounding country districts. This development has up to now simply taken place without any precise, joint supervision of planning in the region of Funen as a whole; but this is being remedied in recent years.

Before we move on to look at the country community we must mention the middle group between market towns and country villages which resulted from the arrival of the railway from 1865 onwards – the station towns. Examples are Ringe on the Odense-Svendborg line, Glamsbjerg on the Assens line and Årup on the Nyborg-Middelfart line, all of which mushroomed around the railway stations. These station towns quickly had their chemist, doctor, savings bank, post office, secondary school, business firms, and semi-skilled craftsmen. In these cases another contributing factor was that they were already situated between the market towns and the periphery of their hinterland areas.

Villages on Funen

by Finn Stendal Pedersen

When one drives through the countryside of Funen the asphalt roads often lead the traveller through built-up areas with low and spread-out clusters of houses which appear curiously gratuitous and straggling when compared to the surrounding countryside and the highly functional strip of road that purposefully forges its way through the buildings. Often, if it is one of the main roads, the motorist's only conscious reaction to the buildings will be a casual irritation at being forced to reduce speed and to show increased attention to other types of road-users, school children and the elderly, who for a brief period threaten traffic safety. Now and then a single petrol pump in front of a local shop bears witness to a slight tribute to the demands of modern times. If one drives slightly off the beaten track and along one of the smaller and twisting secondary roads, one can come across houses in a less straggling version and with a greater degree of uniformity throughout clusters of houses. In both cases one is struck by the well- or less well-preserved remains of an organism that once was alive and functional, the village of Funen.

Today only a small section of the population of Funen lives in a village; economic and technical development have meant that the market towns and station towns, as mentioned previously, have become the totally predominant building and housing areas. In 1970 the total population of Funen with the surrounding islands was altogether 432,699. 317,257 of these lived in built-up areas with at least 200 of a population and c. 240,000 of this number lived in the large market town housing areas. As this method of statistical survey that defines a built-up area as having at least 200 inhabitants differs from the existing

"There were two men in one village, who both had the very same name; they were both called Claus. One of them owned four horses, the other only one ... All through the week Little Claus had to plough for Big Claus and lend him his one horse; in return, Big Claus gave him the help of all his four horses, but only once a week, and that was on Sunday" (from "Hans Christian Andersen's Fairy Tales": *Little Claus and Big Claus*, translated by R. P. Keigwin. Skandinavisk Bogforlag). Drawing by Louis Moe.

conception of a village, by which built-up areas with three farms or over are considered to be a village, it is difficult to give a precise impression of the population division between station towns, solitary farm buildings and village settlements, but less than a quarter of the population today lives in a village. Even though the definite number of inhabitants in these villages is numerically small, the village settlement itself in its present form leaves its mark on the Funen landscape much more forcibly than the population in itself warrants and must be considered as something typical for Funen.

The origins of the Funen village wander off through the Middle Ages and right back to ancient times. The village's entangled journey through time will not be pursued here, but if one is to appreciate the Funen village's structure and significance one must go more than 200 years back. Thus we trace it back to a community that was a distinctly self-supporting and static agricultural community. Some gravelled roads with potholes, often only ruts in the ground, united the individual villages with each other and with the outside world. It was difficult and time-wasting to transport wares and people from place to place.

A third circumstance ought also to be mentioned; that is the fact that it was a society in which modern central administration and public forces of law and order were barely established and not at all organised to reach the separate regional areas. The poor contact that existed between the authorities and the individual inhabitants was often effected by the local landowner or parson, the most important function most definitely being tax-collecting. In 1769, the time of the first population census in Denmark, between 90–95% of the population of Funen lived in self-supporting villages. Whatever need there was for buying and selling wares was satisfied in the nearest market town or at the merchant's or by trading on the statutory market days (if indeed one did not trade with the local landowner); but only a small turn-over was necessary, as the individual villages by and large got through daily life on their own. This means that most of the cultural background that today is considered specially "Funen" has come about and has its roots in the way of living in the Funen village. In Hans Christian Andersen's works the village of Funen also occupies its essential place. Among the fairy tales the following may be mentioned: "The Ugly Duckling", "Numskull Jack" (Simple Simon), "Little Claus and Big Claus", "What the Old Man Does", "The Flax" and "The Buckwheat".

If we now try to imagine the villages as they looked 200

ndborg Station at the turn of the century. Until 1949 Funen had the most closely packed
vork of railways in the whole country, largely consisting of private railways.

the Ice Behind the Town". Town and country scene from Fåborg, painted in 1901 by Peter
sen. (102×164 cm. *Statens Museum for Kunst*).

A half-timbered merchant's house in Assens from 1675, with carved timbers. Now town m
um (Willemoesgården).

Market day. The atmosphere of the old market town is preserved around Sortebrødre Squa
Odense.

tapperstræde (Tapster street) in Odense, a modern shopping precinct that is modelled on the
ling traditions of the ancient market towns.

Ærøskøbing is one of the favourite tourist attractions, thanks to the unusually well-preser_ houses. Here is a glimpse from Søndergade in which the oldest house dates from the _ century.

There are pedestrian precincts in many of the Funen market towns, e.g., here in Fåborg, their number increases in the summer.

...inde Bystævne, one of the old village meeting places, where the inhabitants met to decide on ...y and important affairs. Painting by A. P. Madsen, 1887. (*Nationalmuseet*).

...n today it is possible to find in a few places unspoilt village idylls, as here by the village pond ...yø on the island of Lyø.

A typical small holding. Husby, West Funen.

Voldsgård near Borreby with beautiful half-timber work.

nemøllen (windmill) in the outskirts of Kerteminde was built in 1850. It adds character to the
e, smiling market town, and thanks to the town's famous artist, Johannes Larsen, it is often
trayed in paintings.

byværk watermill by the River Odense in Sønder Broby was an armoury in the 17th century;
e then it was put to a more peaceful use, namely the grinding of corn. It is, as time goes on,
of the few attractive watermills that Denmark has left.

years ago and earlier, then we can immediately understand the siting of the buildings and economic and social functions better than from its appearance today.

The structure of estates and village settlements was the same throughout the Danish kingdom in earlier times, but the lay-out varied from province to province. If we turn to siting of the buildings, we see that a local, rational location for the village was sought, based on the premise that the inhabitants had to live by agriculture. The area and building were coordinated factors of the same economic function. They had to have access to fresh water, fields, pasture land, firewood and building materials within a reasonable distance of the settlement. First and foremost the water supply was a prerequisite for the establishing of a settlement. As far as the collected form of the village settlement was concerned, they were free to exploit the possibilities offered by the terrain in connection with the desire for a collectively organised and regulated settlement lying in the middle of the cultivated ground.

As far as Funen is concerned the villages are to a very large extent placed in connection with river valleys, lakes and marshes, and plateau ridges also attracted settlements, while the large expanses of plain were practically uninhabited. With regard to the construction plan one can distinguish between two basic types:
1) the enclosed village that is situated in the middle of the common fields and in which the buildings are closely packed near each other in a quadrangle, rectangle, oval or

Aerial photograph of the village of Viby (the built-up area in the middle), 1977. One can see how the buildings in Viby still lie close together. In spite of the changes in land distribution from 1798 to today the old roads and hedge divisions are to a large extent still unchanged, so that the structure of the built-up area and the division of acreage appear in a form that closely resembles the structure of the reconstructed village of Harndrup (see page 36).
Photo: Geodetic Institute, Denmark, D 7702 K/895, 1977. Reproduced with permission of the Institute (A. 74/80). Copyright.

square with a well-defined outer limit and enclosing a common green in the centre. This type seems to have been preferred in the completely flat plains where it has not been necessary to take the nature of the terrain into consideration when positioning the buildings, but rather attention is paid to the unity of all the buildings;

2) the open road town in more or less regular formation with the individual farms and houses placed on both sides of a road; this makes it possible for the individual buildings to be placed to their greatest advantage in connection with the landscape, for example to lie sheltered from the wind.

The latter type of building form is mostly found in hilly moraine formations and is without doubt the dominant one on Funen, in contrast to the enclosed village that is the prevalent type east of the Storebælt. Of the c. 1,000 villages that existed in 18th century Funen only a handful can be characterized as being enclosed villages (e.g., Volderslev, Sdr. Nærå, Brudager and Sandager), while the rest can be listed under various types of the open road village. Some typical varieties of open road village on Funen are as follows: the twining road villages (e.g., Østrup, Harndrup, Taarup, Voldtofte, Humble and Viby), towns huddled round the road (e.g., Nr. Broby, Aasum and Skårup) or villages irregularly placed by the road (e.g., Snøde, Hesselager and Fangel). As the number of parishes on Funen amounts to just under 200, there was therefore an average of five of these village communities in every parish.

As mentioned above, the cultivation of the arable area was the common basis for a village's farmers from the Middle Ages until the Enclosure Movement at the end of the 18th century. The three course system was the prevalent agricultural method in east Denmark, i.e., Skåne, Zealand and the surrounding islands. Each village had its common field area that was divided into three major fields. Each of these fields were made up of a number of beams and in it every farm in the village had its "selion" or plot of land. The individual farm's ground was in this way spread out

34

over the entire common field. The basic principle behind this division, it was presumed, was that all farms, no matter the size of the share of the total ground, should have an equal share in both good and poor soil. According to the earliest source material for the statistical information of the structure of the village, an impressive survey and valuation of the individual villages in Christian V's reign (from 1682 as far as Funen was concerned), closer investigation shows however that the distribution of land was not always as equal as the above-mentioned principle suggests. An investigation of the following villages – Allese, Skovshøjrup, Kirkendrup, Broby and Næsby shows quite large deviations (compared with the principles) in the Funen villages.

The rotation in this three course system was: first year normally winter crops, largely rye, second year spring cereal, largely barley and oats, and the third year the field lay fallow, that is it was laid down in grass (the variety that grew by itself). At one given point a third of the village's total field area would be planted with rye or another winter crop, a third with barley or oats and a third laid down in grass. In addition to the above-mentioned cereals a fair bit of buckwheat and peas was often grown on Funen. In addition, uncultivated areas could lie around the cultivated section, and these were divided out amongst a number of villages and used for grazing – the so-called common. The common was however relatively small and rare on Funen. This three course system predominated on Funen in 1682 in an area that roughly corresponded to the previous Svendborg region, while a somewhat different system with many variations dominated in the northern and western part of Funen. An example of this is the village of Harndrup in north-west Funen in the Vends district; it lies in typical, hilly moraine landscape and the village has been described as an open road village. Karl-Erik Frandsen has shown in a reconstruction (see the plan reconstruction on page 36) of the field system in 1682 three major fields, Harnidtz field east of the town, Schou field north of the

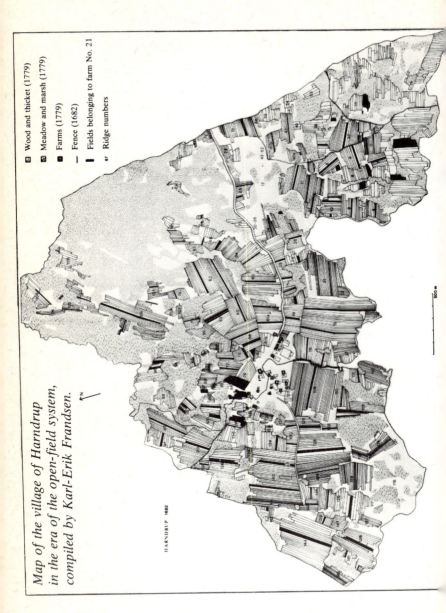

Map of the village of Harndrup in the era of the open-field system, compiled by Karl-Erik Frandsen.

Wood and thicket (1779)

Meadow and marsh (1779)

Farms (1779)

Fence (1682)

Fields belonging to farm No. 21

Ridge numbers

HARNDRUP 1682

500 m

town and Tieridts field west of the town. Two of the fields are shown to have been cultivated for two years and lie fallow for two years, while the third field had an annual crop. The basic principle here, therefore, is a two course system to which a third field is added later that has scarcely been sown every year, but which, because of the hay harvest that had been pretty considerable in this field, the fences have not been opened and the field given over to grazing. In addition to these major fields the town had large cattle yards that were separately enclosed and which were sown for two years and rested for four. The town did not have a common. A number of individually cultivated and separately enclosed yards were spread out around the countryside. Hans Christian Andersen describes in "The Buckwheat" the view of the sown village fields in this way: "On all the meadows round about grew Corn, both Rye, Barley and Oats, yes, the lovely Oats that looks when ripe like a large number of small, gold canarybirds on a branch. The Corn looked so heavenly and the heavier it was the lower it bowed in meek humility. But there was also a meadow with Buckwheat and this meadow was straight ahead of the old willow tree; the Buckwheat did not bow at all like the other corn, it held its head up high, proudly and stiffly."

The ground apportioned to farm 21 is marked in black on the figure of Harndrup. It can be seen from this how widely spread the plots of land belonging to the individual farm lay in the common fields and also how the individual farmers were forced to conform to the whole system as far as ploughing, sowing and harvesting in the separate parts of the common field were concerned. In order to administer the necessary cooperation they had an organisation, the town guild, where the farmers of the village met and at the town convention made the necessary decisions by a majority vote.

The first time that the village's autonomy and authority are clearly acknowledged in Danish legislation is in the

Funen Statutes of 1492. This is what it says in § 16 among other things:

> "Item hwat vidæ som almwe legge vdi noger by eller torp om hegn oc gierde oc andre bysens nytte og tarff, thet maa ey en grannæ eller two kolkaste men skulle alle holde vidæ oc vedertecht".
> (In the same way one or two neighbours must not upset the resolutions that villagers adopt in any town or village concerning hedges, fences and other items in the town's interest, but they shall all respect the decisions and resolutions made).

The oldest preserved statute for a Danish village council dates from the immediately following years, the statutes for the Funen village of Allese that is dated c. 1500. The second oldest preserved statute also comes from Funen, written down in 1559 for the town of Horne. After this date we find a large number of statutes preserved for Funen villages and with the introduction of absolutism in Denmark the villages' autonomy is maintained in Christian V's Danish Law's third book, chapter 13 (3–13–31).

One of the oldest, preserved village statutes on Funen is for the village of Østrup in Lunde district in North Funen. The statute, which is preserved in the Royal Library in Copenhagen, was read and approved at the Lunde moot on Wednesday 16 May, 1598, after a voluntary settlement between the villagers of the time, and when in 1773 at the same moot a dispute between the village farmers on grazing rights was brought to appeal, the provisions of the same statute were cited by the majority of the villagers and in the end formed the basis for the final judgement. This statute, which has therefore been valid for more than 200 years, contains a number of provisions on how the common fences should be maintained and when they should be set up. They also tell how to herd the cattle and how to employ a common village shepherd, the fireplaces must also be inspected so that "evil" ovens do not bring about conflagrations, and a common parish bull is agreed upon. In addition to a number of practical and necessary provisions on the cultivation of the fields, the statutes for Østrup show also how the village was forced into social cooperation in daily life. If a theft were discovered somewhere, the village men had the right to ransack private houses to find the stolen goods; if it was a thief from outside town who had been involved, one was bound to take up the chase together with the injured neighbour, to bring the thief to justice. One was bound to help in illness and to help in the case of death to watch over the body and take part in the funeral.

Infringements of the existing rules are proclaimed at the village convention which is held every Sunday after church, and offences punished with fines, that in the original statutes are usually larger or smaller quantities of beer. One might suspect that the collection and consumption by the village wise men has not always led to a dignified parliamentary debate, at least one of the rules goes as follows: if anyone enjoins the guild master to fight with him at the convention, when he speaks about the town's benefits and advantages, he will be fined an "otting" of beer (c. 16 litres). This guild master was the elected leader of the town council and at the village meetings and this position rotated, in that the period of office was one year at a time. Crofters and tradesmen in the village without land did not have access to the serious debates in the town convention and women also were excluded in general. In addition to the above rules for the daily management and social life of the village, the regulations for Østrup include moreover a so-called celebration custom, the rules for which largely cover the organisation of a large and extensive Whitsun celebration that was a "Dutch treat" and the entire population of the village participated, including crofters and servants, women and children. The economic management cooperation in the village led to a strong social union and it might be mentioned in this connection that this compulsory solidarity has not always been considered agreeable. A rather macabre tradition known in certain villages was that the married women once a year undertook the so-called "milking", i.e., they examined the breasts of the unmarried women to find out if they had given birth clandestinely, as it was called. Neither was it fun to be accused of theft in such a close community from which one could not escape. In the Funen village, therefore, " grass-roots democracy" was practised for centuries within a natural geographical and economic framework.

In the latter half of the 18th century the point was reached at which increased production was desirable, and increased production, according to the economic/political theories of that time, could best be ensured by the abolition of the individual farming family's dependence on agricultural cooperatives, and the village's traditional methods of production besides, so that the individual's interest in increased yield was promoted. In the 25 years from 1781–1806 the entire village community described above was broken up, a fundamental social revolution therefore occurred by the replacement of the community. This replacement was the enclosure system by which the land of the individual farms was collected together in 3 places at the most. By the enclosure system one had the chance to fence in and run the separate farm's land independently of the neighbours, so that technical advances and soil improvement could be exploited by the individual farmer. In this way farm number 21 in Harndrup by the enclosure system had its land collected in one place. The fact that the enclosure system in the long run created more problems than it solved, will not be examined here, but in the wake of the system came the scattering of farms to the newly apportioned land from the farms and houses lying in the village and thereby there again occurred a break-down of the old social rules and regulations. The community was replaced by individualism, but the removals and the termination of the old customs of living together occurred considerably more slowly than the enclosure system itself. On Funen they were reluctant to scatter the farms, so, although there was in the course of 200 years a slow erosion of the existing villages, they were however preserved in greater

40

"The other son had learnt up all the by-laws of the city companies and the things every alderman is supposed to know; he thought this would help him to talk politics with the Princess; and, besides, he knew how to embroider braces, he was so very clever with his fingers . . . "So these are the gentry?" said Simon. "Well, here's one for the alderman!" And he turned out his pocket and let him have the mud full in the face" (from "Hans Christian Andersen's Fairy Tales": *Simple Simon,* translated by R. P. Keigwin. Skandinavisk Bogforlag). Drawing by Hans Tegner.

number than in other places in the country, a unique example being the village of Viby on Hindsholm that did not embrace the enclosure system.

During the 19th century the increase of the population further led to the fact that a number of smaller houses without land in the villages were built instead of the farms that had been moved out to their newly apportioned land outside the community. These houses, which were often

41

occupied by the day-labourers and elderly retired farmers, helped fill in the gaps that had arisen in the housing and preserve the uniform character of the housing. A number of villages became also at the end of the 19th century the home of new, common activities. School buildings were largely placed in the villages. In connection with religious movements throughout the entire 19th century new buildings, "meeting halls" were built often within the individual parishes, for meetings and other cultural activities. Later with the breakthrough of the cooperative movement there followed the building of dairies, feedstuff companies and cooperative stores. Usually only one cooperative store was built in every parish, so that only about 20% of the old villages were given in this way a new significance as a local centre for both the existing village and the separate farms and houses that had been moved out in the specific parish. This was a new economic and cultural activity that in the Danish tradition represents one of the most significant aspects in democratic progress and which only in recent decades had been forced to be on the defensive.

The native of Funen does not seem to be attracted by the big city life, as was mentioned in the section on the Market towns; the way of living and forms of cooperating, the functional basis of which disappeared 200 years ago, have cropped up again in recent times from a desire to recreate "the intimate society" that existed in former times.

In the report on alternative outlines for regional planning for the region of Funen, the officials employ three improvement alternatives for the area, one of which is called the village alternative. If one examines the report more closely one can see that the problem first and foremost concerns a solution to the siting of industry and administration (service trades), while the residential area is broadly speaking not altered by the planning. If one looks at the actual siting of places of work in the village alternative, it appears that they are indeed more decentralised than in the other alternatives, but nevertheless are collected in local centres to which the people must go from the residential areas. This is no real case of the recreation of the old village structure with its economic and social interdependence, but simply a vivid example of the most decentralised plan. One has to acknowledge, therefore, that the earlier connection between economic structure and housing form in the villages cannot be recreated, but on the other hand the site of the buildings and the pattern of the siting of the houses in an imitation of village surroundings could occur, no matter which improvement alternative is chosen. Such a practical and realistic attempt to create an intimate society as far as housing is concerned is happening with the development planning of the village of Andebølle. They have tried to plan a new village beside the old one in such a way that the siting of the buildings in relation to the landscape and road system makes allowances for the same aesthetic values of experience that the study of the old village revealed. It says in a practical way in the report "one can learn from the old villages, but one must not copy them, and their housing. One must not bring about an impossible dream by jumping back to the 18th and 19th centuries and one must not build ill-judged historical replicas with false half-timber work and arched windows, thatch and farm house romance. Neither can one hope to recreate all the lively activity that characterized the old towns. The many small workshops and small traders that brought life to the town will hardly return."

It is the old, common, worth-while features, the look of a town, the houses in relation to each other, the trees, quickset hedges, the look of the road and its course, that is needed to create an interesting town.

But in this way one also creates an intimate society with the social happinesses and problems it brings. In as much as one can recreate the village atmosphere in new villages, which affords aesthetically rich experience with a reasonable and residential function in an "intimate" society, the Funen village as a housing area may have a renaissance, even though the original foundations for the community belong to the past. Let us conclude this survey of the Funen village's past and future with the following quotation from Arent Berntsen's work of 1656 "Denmark's and Norway's fertile splendour": "Funen is rightly considered to be the most dignified and best of the Danish islands, after Zealand, both by its situation and its splendid nature and conditions, therefore it is not unfitting that it maintains that it has its name from the word 'fine', and the inhabitants call everything FINE which they think beautiful and charming."

Architecture

by Gorm Benzon

It is but natural to begin an exposition of the architecture of Funen with the oldest buildings, the churches, the great majority of which are built in the 12th century. The first construction material was wood, of which there was enough in the extensive forests. At a very early time, however, the churches were made of stone, perhaps because one had realized that wooden buildings rarely stood for terribly long in the Danish climate and that to the south, where the new religion came from, the churches were practically without exception built of stone.

The Danish king, St Knud (–1086) used tufa stone when he commenced the building of the church in Odense which later came to bear his name – St Knud's Church. Tufa stone is formed when calcerous springs break out from the earth and the chalk is deposited around straw, moss, leaves, snails, roaches, etc. The deposits can be found in rather thick strata and the stone is remarkable for being very soft and fresh, so that with the proper tools it can be fashioned in blocks of adequate size. When the blocks are allowed to lie and dry in the sun they become hard and insoluble in water. If you look at the surface of tufa stone you can see in it signs of the straw, leaves, etc. which at one time were embedded in the calcerous silt.

In the region of Funen there are only eight churches in which tufa stone has been used as the principal material, or in which this stone is found as an important secondary material; this is the case, for example, in Hesselager Church.

Although Denmark is poor in raw materials, yet there is one thing there has always been lots of, namely large granite boulders. They have made life extremely difficult for farmers, as they got in the way of their work in the fields, but as building material, for both dikes and masonry, they proved to be first-class. In the Romanesque period it was granite in many parts of the country – including Funen – that was the material chosen for church construction. About 136 churches on Funen have granite as the major building material.

It was a time-consuming and demanding process to fashion the boulders to smooth ashlars. It was easiest to take some as they were and split others. In this way one got an interplay between rounded off and sharp-edged stones, which, when carefully positioned, provided a very stable and non-slip construction. The meticulous inhabitants of Funen largely chose to build this mixture of materials on a base of dressed ashlar, often two courses high with chamfered edges, and they preferred to place ashlars in the corners. This increased the stability and gave the building a tidy look. It is also not rare to see the ashlar corners removed when, for example, the church was expanded in the late Gothic period. Such is the case with Vedtofte Church on West Funen.

In other cases the churches are built partly of ashlar and partly of rough and split granite. Thus the choir, the holiest part, in *Hjadstrup Church* on North Funen, is built of ashlar, while the nave is of the more rustic rough and split granite.

Figure-ashlar is found in the Romanesque granite stone churches and such shaped stone is included in some churches on Langeland, Ærø and Funen, but they rarely reach the stature of what in that respect is achieved in Jutland. Funen is said to display, however, Denmark's most beautiful figure-stone; it is a representation of an angel performing on a stringed instrument. Along with other figure-stones and fragments of them it is set into the wall of the chancel of *Gamtofte Church* on West Funen and they all originate from a now ruined apse which must have been of marvellously dignified artistic quality.

This remarkable granite relief expresses the music of Heaven. It is to be found in the wall of Gamtofte Church in West Funen. This sculpture (height almost a metre) represents an angel who is playing a stringed instrument. It dates from the last decades of the 12th century and may be a fragment of a larger work. Here reproduced from a stone-rubbing by Mr. Ib Stubbe Teglbjærg.

Very striking and distinctive is also a figure-stone found at the foot of the south-facing door of *Ørsted Church*. It shows a soldier with sword and shield in battle with a ferocious lion and the following inscription is carved in runes:

47

"Eskild i gaard skar Samson; han dræbte løven!" (Eskild in Gaard – the stonemaster – cut the figure of Samson, who killed the animal). *Snøde Church* has a lovely carved stone of a man who represents either the archangel Michael weighing souls or David with the sling. There is also a soldier, a lion and a fish on the figure-ashlar.

Rise Church on Ærø displays a tympanum (lintel) over a bricked up priest's door with three heads, a lion, a dragon and two limestone reliefs with a hunter with hound and wild boar.

Bricks came to Denmark in the 12th century. As it was monks who began their manufacture, they were called "monks' stone". Their smallest size is $27 \times 12 \times 8$ cm. Gradually bricks, which were originally considered supplementary material, became largely used in areas that had few suitable granite boulders, such as Lolland and Falster, whereas Funen, that was rich in unhewn stone, only has 22 romanesque brick churches. The most interesting of these is *Dalum Abbey Church* whose oldest sections go back to around the year 1200 and in which a splendid late romanesque interior is preserved in the northern transept. *St Nicolai Church* in Svendborg also contains architecture of great interest. It appears in a great many ways to be a late romanesque basilica; the oldest section appears to have been built before the middle of the 13th century. It is greatly influenced by contemporary north German ecclesiastic architecture and most unusual is the patterned brickwork found on the chancel wall. To the north are represented practically all the late romanesque ornamental courses; it appears as if the brickwork was done according to a regulation manual in a school-book for masons or architects.

Romanesque churches nearly all had horizontal beamed ceilings and a church tower was a rare sight. Most places made do with a bell frame or a detached bell building. In *Kerte Church* on West Funen they adhered to the rule that bell-ringing should take place away from the church itself,

ælager Church which in the Renaissance was given Italian gables with elegant curves.

ɔw: (left) Ullerslev Church, the core of which is preserved and built of dressed and undressed
ite boulders; (right) Svindinge Church, one of Denmark's few, sterling Renaissance
ches.

The crypt of St Knud's Church with St Knud's shrine.

A detail of Claus Berg's altarpiece in St Knud's Church; figures at the base of the altar. (*Nationalmuseet*)

Opposite: St Knud's Church, Odense. Nave and chancel. ▶

Horne Church, the oldest part of which, the central part of the nave, is one of Denmark's se
remaining circular churches.

Skovby Church on North Funen is a majestic structure; the chancel and apse and part of the n
were built in the Romanesque period of granite ashlar.

org Castle, in spite of its impressive dimensions, is only part of fortifications that were one of kingdom's most important and strongest well into the Middle Ages. Below: Interior.

Hesselagergaard, built in the years 1538–50, is one of Denmark's most remarkable houses

Rygaard by Langå on East Funen – a small, medieval baronial castle.

...skov Castle, the magnificent Renaissance island fort in Mid-Funen. Below: Living-room ...rior.

Krengerup Castle, flanked by its homefarm buildings. An imposing design of the neo-class
period.

As a relic of the Middle Ages Østrupgaard is situated on its small castle mound surrounded
marvellous half-timbered homefarm.

but they still wanted a church tower, hence the detached, late Gothic church tower (Denmark's only one of that period) was built. The plan of the typical romanesque church was a nave, a narrower chancel and an even narrower apse in which the communion table was placed. Altarpieces were not common in those days, not until the gothic period. The most widespread was a very low and broad altarpiece with two wings to open and shut it, but there was rarely place for them in the apse, therefore in many places they chose to demolish the apse. When they were doing that it was very convenient at the same time to extend the chancel, so that it became a continuation of the nave's masonry and in that way some space was gained. Thus "nave churches" came into being, e.g., *Skovby Church*.

Gradually all the old Funen churches had towers, most of them at the west, but there are exceptions to this rule. Normally the older church towers on Funen are very stocky, more so than those in Jutland, and the fact that certain individual churches, e.g., *Ore Church* in North Funen, has a rather slender tower is probably due to the fact that the terrain could not bear a larger affair. Many churches have corbie gables and especially in West Funen one finds on top of the corbie steps pinnacles – small spires.

Marvellous niche decorations can be seen on the gables of the chancel, tower gables and porches, and wherever there had been space for them. On some churches the amount of niches can be quite overpowering. One should also mention the native of Funen's love of the saw-tooth course, brickwork that looks like the teeth of a sawblade. The craftsmen made use of it wherever there was an opportunity, e.g., *Ubberup Church* tower has many bands with saw-tooth courses, which gives it an extremely special effect.

The romanesque churches did not have an abundance of vaulting; by far the majority of naves and chancels had horizontal beamed ceilings, or, more seldom, open roof trusses. It does occur, however, that an apse has a half-domed vault, which is, all things considered, a quarter ball socket. There was enough to support such a vault on all sides, so it was not extremely complicated to build.

In addition to the half-domed vault could be found barrel-vaulting and finally groin-vaulting, in which two barrel-vaults cut across each other and meet in the groin.

Until c. 1200 these were the only possible types of ceiling and only half-domed vaults are to be seen in Funen churches of the romanesque period. Meanwhile they learned to build ribbed vaulting and in that way high constructions reaching to the heavens could be built. The ribs that stretch from corner to corner and are supported by corbels, pillars or miniature columns, could bear fairly broad and high vaults. From the 15th century these ribbed vaults were made more varied, so that the ribs create by and large a pattern of stars and naturally are called star-vaulting.

Surprisingly many master masons on Funen found it very difficult to construct these star-vaults and, e.g., in *Bovense Church* near Middelfart, they got by with simply sticking the stars on the completed ribbed vaulting. The Funen region has 34 purely Gothic brick churches, of which one is on Langeland and the rest on the main island. Most attractive of all is *St Knud's Church* in Odense, which is nearly the only large Danish church which, after its reconstruction in the 13th century, completely fulfils the gothic ideal. The interior with its high, contoured pillars and arcades with pointed arches that divide the principal nave from the side aisles and the elegant ribbed-vaults are all of a quality that is not normally reached in Denmark, or rather that has not been preserved. It very often occurred that the brick work could not support the pressure of the vaulting alone, so it was necessary to strengthen it with ordinary straight or sloping pillars, so-called buttresses – that stand up against the wall. In basilicas, as St Knud's Church is, for example, the walls of the side aisle are to a certain extent made into a sort of buttress construction, but that alone cannot bear the enormous weight of the high vault, so it is supplemented by buttresses along the outside of the wall. The pressure is taken away from the church in this way and led down to the earth, so that not only is the weight taken off the brick work and pillars inside the church, but also the whole building is firmly fixed, one might say, and locked together. Ordinary struts are found in a large number of churches on Funen; more interesting are, however, flying buttresses; the struts are built in the form of an arch, so that it meets the wall on a very limited surface and takes the strain of a vault at this point.

Among the later additions to St Knud's Church should be mentioned Christian III's tower of 1558, the spire of which was renewed in 1783–85, thus simplifying it somewhat. On the north side of the nave there was erected a late Renaissance chapel in 1631–34 with elegantly sweeping gables. The gate of the chapel inside the church is no less magnificent – a wrought iron gate executed by Christian IV's artistic smith Caspar Fincke. The Ahlefeldt Chapel should also be named, with its sumptuous coffins, funeral armour and sepulchral tablets in white and black marble by Denmark's greatest baroque sculptor, Thomas Quellinus. An extremely curious design is found in *Vor Frue Kirke* (Our Lady's Church) in Assens, in which a romanesque church is swallowed up by a late gothic building that was completed in 1488. The porch is an addition of c. 1500, but the so-called Holevad Chapel is earlier than the rest of the church, that is, from the beginning of the 15th century. The tower which rests on an older, square base, is remarkable in that it is octagonal and is Denmark's only octagonal medieval church tower.

In the Renaissance there were even fewer churches built than in the Gothic period. *Svindinge Church* on East Funen belongs to the few truly Renaissance churches that Denmark can boast of at all. Outwardly it has, however, mainly a gothic look.

The most important occurrence as far as construction was concerned was undoubtedly the fact that a number of churches were given what is called Italian gables with elegant curves. The most distinctive of these without doubt is *Hesselager Church* where the kingdom's powerful chancellor, Johan Friis of Hesselagergaard, amongst other things, had the chancel gable decorated. It was given curved edges and an incredible wealth of niches. On the nearby Hesselagergaard there are gables that resemble them, but they do not quite match them and the chancel gable is without doubt the more splendid. The gables on the side chapels are less lavish repetitions of this masterpiece which was undoubtedly instigated by King Christian III's master builder, Morten Bussert.

One cannot claim that the region of Funen is Denmark's richest in wall-paintings, but a number of excellent examples can be pointed out. Late romanesque painting is found in the chancel of *Sanderum Church,* showing, *inter alia* the Prophets and scenes from the Book of Ruth and the Book of Numbers, with the scouts who come home from the land of Canaan with bunches of grapes. The church has also a number of late gothic paintings with, amongst others, Christ's Passion, St Michael as dragon-slayer, St Christopher with the child Jesus and the holy family.

Sønder Nærå Church has frescoes from around 1200 which were however severely damaged by the vaults built in at a later date. Of interest is the painting of a young man with a sword and a ring and a young woman with a lily – the symbol of virginity. A heraldic shield of the Eberstein or Gleichen family, both of whom belong to the Danish medieval nobility, are reproduced.

Among late gothic wall paintings one can name *Bellinge Church's* very lively representation, in which, amongst others, a knight in armour and a lur-blowing fool are marvellous. *Dalum Church* has also late gothic paintings with a single motif of a supposedly bold nature. The northern transept of *Søndersø Church* has very beautiful paintings

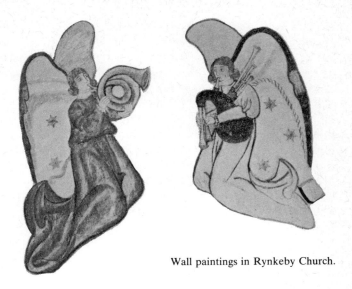

Wall paintings in Rynkeby Church.

amongst which is one of the Virgin Mary as Queen of
Heaven, Mary worshipping the child Jesus and the Adora-
tion of the Magi. An extremely lovely Annunciation painting is also included. *Bregninge Church* on Ærø is quite
rightly well-known for its fine late gothic frescoes with,
among others, an elegant representation of Salome's dance.
Others include Christ as Judge of the World, his flagella-
tion and the crowning with thorns as well as his Ascension.
There is also an unusual fool's head.

Gislev Church has late gothic paintings with, amongst
others, the Passion and scenes from Christ's birth and life.
Langaa Church is distinguished by its reproduction of Pilate washing his hands and Pilate is given the face of the
Danish king Christian II who had to flee in exile. *Ørbæk
Church* has some curious, very naive pictures of animals,
people and symbols – all done in a very primitive style.

Finally *Rynkeby Church* must be mentioned, where in
1964 there was found in the north chapel some quite exceptional frescoes from the period around 1560 – i.e. the

Renaissance – and show an entire angelic orchestra, 32 angels in all with instruments. It is famous today all over the world amongst music historians as this is considered to be the most detailed and richest representation of Renaissance musical instruments.

It is outside the scope of this exposition to include the fabric and furnishings of the church, but it must be mentioned that there are very beautiful, romanesque granite fonts in many of the churches on Funen, e.g., the font in *Kullerup Church* which is decorated with lions and men's heads, and that in *Melby Church* has a square base and with its double acanthus ring shows close relationship with the font art of Djursland. The Søndersø font, however, has figures of the mid-Funen type with an enthroned Christ, St Peter and probably Paul, as well as a double-headed eagle, animal figures and plant ornamentation.

Ørslev Church has also an unusual font; it consists of a large soapstone vessel from the Viking period, undoubtedly originally a pagan sacrificial vessel, which is loosely placed on a romanesque granite capital. The font in *Uggerslev Church* should also be mentioned, as it has been imported from Gotland and made of limestone around 1350. The octagonal bowl has reliefs of curious, fabulous creatures. Another font from Gotland is in *Ellinge Church*. Master Sighrafr has depicted on the bowl the childhood of Jesus in eight motifs. Finally we can mention Master Hvicmann's fonts in *Åstrup* and *Hillerslev Churches*. The latter has reliefs on the bowl of Christ with blessing gesture placed between Peter and another saint, and at the foot are men and lions fighting.

The most important woodcarver in the Middle Ages in Denmark, the north German Claus Berg, worked here in Denmark from c. 1500–1532 and made altarpieces, crucifixes and other furnishings for a number of churches on Funen. His greatest altarpiece is found in St Knud's Church in Odense. It was originally donated by King Hans's queen, Christine, to *Gråbrødrekirken* (Franciscan church), but when it was pulled down in 1885 the altarpiece was taken to St Knud's Church. This brilliantly carved piece, rich in figures, is one of Europe's most splendid examples of late gothic carving. Claus Berg was the master carver of many altarpieces, crucifixes, etc. in churches on Funen, among others the Assumption altarpiece and a crucifix in *Vindinge Church* as well as a crucifix and pulpit in *Thurø Church*.

From the church itself we shall proceed into the churchyard. There are many beautiful, late medieval churchyard portals, for example at Skovby and Gelsted in North Funen. Connected with the churchyard is the tithe-barn which often was later converted to a hospital. There are medieval tithe-barns at Skaarup, Holevad, Mesinge, Revninge, Seden and Vindinge. Hesselager Church's tithe-barn must be extremely old, possibly Denmark's oldest house.

One might expect to find a number of timber-frames in the churches, but this is certainly not the case; every single half-timbered annexe has disappeared, and only two churches, Vantinge and Viby, have timber-frame towers. Vantinge's tower is dated at the beginning of the 17th century, while Viby's is as late as 1718. It has only half-timbered frame above the height of the roof, the rest is stone-built and constructed above the vestry. With its hipped roof and ridge turret it is, however, extremely picturesque.

Otherwise Funen is the part of Denmark that can muster the greatest number of excellent examples of half-timbered buildings; even humble folks' houses and insignificant outhouses use timber in extravagant compactness and of quite impressive dimensions on display. And it had to be oak – nothing else would do. It was well known that the farmers of Funen were not afraid of paying large sums to build their farms, but on the other hand they could procrastinate for a long time with the building. When at the end of the 18th century and beginning of the last century the farms had to be moved from the old open field system of agriculture, the people of Funen were among the very last to move; it could easily be very expensive, you see, when a house had to be properly built.

There is much in common between the timber-framed buildings in east Jutland and on Funen, though one can perhaps say that the type on Funen is more often more systematic and not so varied. On the other hand the timber-framed buildings of Zealand and Funen are not very alike, and even in the forest areas on Zealand the timber-framed buildings are surprisingly austere.

In the early Middle Ages, when there was an abundance of magnificent building timber to be found all over Funen, log houses were chiefly built, that is a plank construction, by which the planks are partly notched into each other, partly into the bearing uprights and beams. Later the abundance of timber thinned out and one had to make do with a framework of uprights and beams, while the surfaces between these – the panels – were filled with clay on wattle made of hazel twigs between slightly thicker rods. The people of Funen apparently did not want to renounce the richness of wood completely and so, between the load-bearing structures – the struts – which were often placed close to each other, a wealth of more or less necessary filling timber was used. It was found in many places, for example, that every upright should have a little brace – a cross-brace – on both sides; first it was mortised in the binding wooden frame – the sill that lies on the foundation stone – and from there into the upright. Between the uprights at window height are inserted horizontal pieces of timber, called intertie, and the cross-braces end just under them. It was also possible instead to place á little brace – a poppet – between the end of the large braces, right in the middle of the panel.

In the row of large panels, in which the windows were placed, it was not the custom to put filling timber, but if there was a row also of intertie above window level, before one reached the timber construction that bears the rafters –

56

the heads – there could also be room for a row of poppets there. This construction can run round the house like a band, but in the gables where the wooden frame continues higher up, there are usually some larger panels above this band of compact timber.

The half-timbered houses in the countryside of Funen usually have hipped gables, that is, the roof in the gable slopes slightly down. On west Funen there is a special type of roof construction, the so-called pillar-construction; the pillars are extremely high timbers attached to the foundation stone in a row throughout the house. They are duly supported by other timber constructions, so they do not tip over. The oldest pillars were tree trunks with stout branch forks; they were debarked and put into position and a very heavy beam – a so-called purlin beam – was used, so it rested on all the boles. Above this purlin beam rafters were positioned with strong pegs and the other end of the rafter rested on the heads (the timber that bears the rafters). In fact we are really talking about a suspended roof.

The wall of a half-timbered house is not very thick and must be built with care if it is to be strong. So it is necessary to have extra safety constructions if it is to withstand storms. On many farmhouses on Funen storm anchors or straps can be seen. There are braces between two panels and, whereas the storm anchor on west Funen farms supports the corner braces themselves, on east and mid-Funen they are attached to the brace next to the outermost one. That provided, so they said, greater elasticity. The same kind of storm anchors were often also placed beside the gateways.

From the one longitudinal wall to the other runs a row of rafters that are mortised into the braces so as not to weaken the heads; a projection runs from them right through the brace and a bit out on the other side. It is locked to the brace by putting one or two strong pegs crossways into it.

This largely is how the long house of Funen was built and the half-timbered houses in the towns do not greatly differ from them in principle. Sometimes they are simply richer and especially in the Renaissance and the early baroque period, the cross rafters, the ceiling joists, rest on corbels – brackets – that were mortised into them and into the braces. These brackets could be carved in different ways or contoured and the strut on each side of the braces could be allowed to extend along with them, so that instead of an open timber construction there appeared a triangular block, that was carved with a marvellous fan-shaped rosette that was naturally painted in bright colours.

There are many manor houses that are half timbered, but not one with as rich decoration; why should this be? The reason is that only the nobility at that time were allowed to build stone houses, and, because of the fire risk, they preferred stone to timber. Commoners were also forbidden to own estates for ages. Even though a merchant was just as rich, he could not build a stone house and he could not invest his money in land. He therefore used his money to build half-timbered houses so that all could see that here indeed lived a man who had authority, so the house had to be decorated accordingly. There was terrific competition to see who could build most strikingly. There are only faint traces today of the fact that the towns of Funen had once been magnificent to look at.

In those days the wood was painted with colouring that was stirred into buttermilk and in that way it was well cemented. This process was called »at afstolpe« (to draw up the timber), and it was done every second year. The panels were allowed to remain white, but one could also limewash them yellow, and, especially in west Funen, they chose to have the lower row yellow and the upper one white. Brown, browny-purple or black best suited the woodwork. In addition pointing could be painted on with light blue, just as on a brick wall. In other places the house is limewashed a red colour and had white or light blue pointing, and particularly in south Funen and the islands they liked to edge the panels, especially when they were white, with light blue and have black timbers. There are however other possibilities, and they are all a relic of the Renaissance that delighted in colours.

Gradually the mud-and-wattle in the panels was replaced with unfired bricks which lasted very well, if whitewashed regularly. Eventually the unfired bricks were only used most places in indoor dividing walls and real bricks placed in the timber frame. The base was tarred, so that its strong smell would keep off small fry.

Doors on Funen are a story in themselves. The main door, the welcoming place of the house, was made a lot of in many places. It is painted in many colours, while the mouldings and contours are meticulously painted, so that they really stand out and add character to the door. Window frames and sash bars are also sometimes brilliantly painted.

A number of old half-timbered farms have round or cut-off corners where the wings come together, and sometimes all the wings are built together to form a square. The only entrance to the farmyard was through the gateway, that was placed in one of the longitudinal walls or, just as often, one of the rounded corners. It was locked in the evening, and as all doors, hatches and windows faced the yard, the system functioned like a little fortress, which in the old and uncertain times might well have had a certain significance.

At one time Funen was an island of mills. Today they have been greatly thinned out, but there are water mills at Lindved, *Røde Mølle* (Red Mill) in Langesø, and further mills in Solevad, Tverskov, Rødkilde and Ventepose, the latter being on Tåsinge. *Lille Mølle* (Little Mill) in Refsvindinge and Kaleko Mill near Fåborg are still functioning, the latter serves also as a museum.

Among the wind mills one might name Stegø and Langø pump mills in the Gyldensteen estate in north Funen,

59

Lydinge, that has both wind and water mills, Egeskov Mill, which was depicted on the old Danish ten crown note, and Dyrehave Mill at Nyborg.

Lovely old vicarages are to be found, for example, in Dalby, Egense, Kølstrup, Horne, Jordløse, Tved, Særslev, Tarup and Sønder Nærå. Attractive farms can also be seen around the island, but the modernisation of agriculture has unfortunately made their continuation to a large extent difficult. The old farming surroundings can be found, for example, at Hjemstavnsgård in Gummerup and in the Open Air Museum »Den fynske Landsby« (the Funen Village) near Odense.

One can no longer find real royal palaces on the island. *Odense Castle* has now been made into public offices and what remains of Nyborg Castle is a museum. Although Odense Castle looks like baroque design, it does include both the remains of a medieval monastery dedicated to St John of Jerusalem, and a Renaissance royal estate, Odensegaard.

Medieval *Nyborg Castle* was extremely dilapidated and greatly reduced in size before large-scale renovations were carried out from 1917–23. At one time the king met here the country's great nobles and a two-storey romanesque palace of about 1265 forms part of the still-preserved building, the king's wing. Around 1470 the castle was extended towards the south and another floor added to it. In the 1540s there were extensions made to the northern part, and the north tower, which was originally on the surrounding walls, became built into the castle itself. In addition a large stair-tower was built, Strange's Tower, out to the courtyard. Christian III's master builder, Morten Bussert, was responsible for the rebuilding, and he equipped the castle with sweeping gables, like those now found in Hesselagergaard. Unfortunately this tower was among one of the sections of the building that was pulled down, after the castle was no longer of strategic importance. Today most of the king's wing remains and has some interesting interiors and two corner towers; the lower part of the once magnificent Knud's Tower which was resplendent with a tall spire is also left, along with a part of the surrounding ramparts and moats.

Brahetrolleborg castle church has remains from the thirteenth century and in the three wings of the castle are still preserved significant parts of a Cistercian monastery of the 15th century. Extensive conversions were made to the south and east wings during the Renaissance, namely, in 1568 and 1620. In 1768 the design was modified according to the dictates of the period, but it was not until 1868–71 that real damage was done, when a roughly handled and unfortunate restoration took place, for example by cement plastering the walls and other important changes to the exterior. At the same time the church was furnished with a neo-gothic spire. In spite of this, Brahetrolleborg can be included amongst our very beautiful manors that are undoubtedly well-worth seeing.

The small *Rygaard* with its four wings, south of Nyborg, is Europe's best preserved, late gothic castle from the age of chivalry. It is certainly no royal castle, but a nobleman's residence, built between 1525 and 1535. The tall main wing at the north was built first, then the gate wing facing it, and finally the two wings were joined together with side wings on the east and west sides. Around 1590 two round stair towers were built, one in the middle of the main building onto the courtyard and the other in the south-west corner of the courtyard. The entrance to the quite small courtyard is through a square gate tower built into the south wing. The floor horizontal divisions in the north and south wings are marked by a curved frieze and at the top of the north wing there juts out a watchman's floor, held up by corbels and with curved recesses which contain machicolations. In the wall there are naturally a very large number of embrasures, and the thick brickwork conceals many secret passages.

From 1776 until recent times the castle was uninhabited,

which was its saving factor. It avoided having large renovations, and when in 1915 and 1922 a thorough-going restoration took place, it was done with true respect for the august house. With its tiny courtyard, from where one looks up to small, old, wrinkled windowpanes, with the corkscrew staircases of the towers, the beautiful late gothic recesses and corbie steps of the gable, this castle is like something out of a fairy tale. Rygaard is the oldest so-called »castle-manors« which used to be plentiful in Denmark, but of which there remain only one on Zealand and five on Funen.

Not far from Rygaard is *Hesselagergaard* which was built in the years 1538–50. It is one of Denmark's most remarkable houses. The upper floor and watchman's storey right on top lean pronouncedly out over the lower floor, so that the house is quite a bit broader at the top than it is at the bottom. The watchman's storey is supported by granite corbels and has of course both machicolations and embrasures. The towers in the corners of the north side are both octagonal and have a little spire, and though they were originally a little higher than now, they have always been lower than the steeply rising house and are quite dominated by the sweeping gables with their lavish recesses. The stair tower is square, but with a round top and contoured openings. Hesselagergaard is best visited in the mists of the autumn and from one of its short sides. When it looms up, self-assured and massive in the mist and wreathed with flaming leaves, it appears like an enormous red bull. Once you have seen this you really know what power means.

And yet Hesselagergaard has no side wings and is not so very big. The same is the case with *Nakkebølle* built in 1559. It is situated near the sea between Svendborg and Fåborg, but is unfortunately not so well-preserved. There are two square corner towers to the south and to the north is a stair-tower that is so broad and deep that it is almost a little side wing. Unfortunately the house was made lower around 1710 and the gables rebuilt. The restoration work in the 1870s in which the corner towers were given Renaissance gables of »sandstone« details from the cementmoulder with flourishes and elaborations did not make good the damage that had been done.

Ørbæklunde west of Nyborg had originally a single wing. The main building was probably commenced in the middle of the 16th century, but was not finished before 1593. The entrance is through an octagonal stair-tower that is built quite far into the house. It goes right up to the roof ridge and is topped by a marvellous lantern, from which there is the most exquisite view over east Funen and in clear weather right over to Zealand. The house is made of red brick on top of a high base of granite blocks and, like the other manor houses, Ørbæklunde has a corbelled storey with embrasures and machicolations on top. The gables are in the most elevated Renaissance style, elegant and sweeping and with a band of sandstone. On the north side are two strong corner-towers as well as a smaller annexe like a bay – a secret, a toilet of that era. The side wing which is rather lower is from 1635, later being somewhat extended. New investigations have however confirmed that the building has been built on medieval foundations to all appearances. A part of the home farm with the stately barn, into which it was possible to drive with a horse and cart, is brick built and dated at 1630.

Europe's best preserved Renaissance island fort is *Egeskov,* one of the most magnificent and best designed houses to be found.

It is strongly influenced by the Renaissance that came to Denmark in the middle of the 16th century. The castle is a double house built in the middle of a little lake and therefore is built on piles of thick oak trunks. The walls rise directly from the water of the moat and to the east two thick, round corner-towers soar, while to the west is a solid, square stair-tower with a spire, a ridge turret, placed on its roof. Egeskov is one of the few places of which it can be said that a restoration, in which certain changes were made, has absolutely made an improvement. In 1881 the gate-house was built by the Swedish architect Helgo Zetterwald, and in 1884 they began on the main building. The work lasted for two years, and the towers were made higher and given spires with garrets and the gables appeared with battlements and niches as well as pinnacles on the ridges.

During recent years the castle has undergone interior restoration during which the owner has been careful to restore the old, Renaissance character of the interior, so that the large and stately great hall was reestablished and it is good to know that it is often opened to the public in connection with cultural arrangements.

There is also timber-frame work in the manors on Funen, and again we are lucky to have a trump card in our hand, that cannot be beaten anywhere in Europe. *Østrupgaard* north of Fåborg is a small, late gothic stone house, lying on a high rampart surrounded by water. On to this is attached a half-timbered wing of the 18th and early 19th centuries. In the neighbourhood of the main building complex is an impressive home farm made completely of timber work and with a thatched roof. Only the dairy wing is brick, built in the last century – all the rest is from the 18th century, e.g., a marvellous stately barn dated at 1742. Up to 50 years ago this type of home farm could be seen in many places, but, as far as is known, this is the only one that is completely preserved. The main building of *Steensgaard* near Millinge is very large and striking, in additon to being extremely old. Parts of the central wing, which at one time stood by itself, are from the end of the 15th century. It is made up of different materials – largely rough boulders were used, but, for example, around the doors and windows large bricks are found. The highest floor is closely timbered; this section probably is from c. 1550, as are also the side-wings. The portals on the main building and the gate-house in the home farm – the so-called German tower – were built in the 1630s.

Just south of Odense are two important half-timbered

kenhavn near Nyborg has rich and elaborate decorations made of pure brickwork.

klunde – a castle of the Danish Renaissance.

Lykkesholm with its gate-tower. The part of the main building in view was built by Domin
Baetiaz.

Funen baroque. The main building on the Brahesborg estate on West Funen.

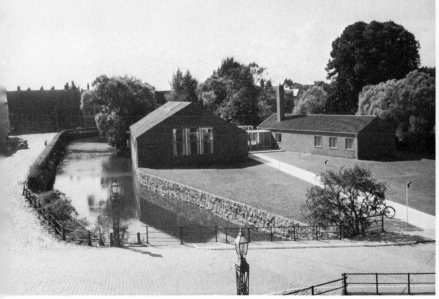

The following illustrations give examples of modern Danish architecture.

Above: (left) Fredens Church, Odense (1916–20), designed by the architect P. V. Jensen Klint; (right) Faaborg Museum (1912–15), designed by professor Carl Petersen.

Below: The Public Library, Nyborg (1938–40). Architects Flemming Lassen and Erik Møller.

The Nursing Home Provstegårdshjemmet, Odense. Architects A. and E. Eriksen.

The Svendborg School Course Centre, designed by architect Oluf Rasmussen, built by S (Specialised Workers' Union in Denmark).

ing Home, Bogense. Architect Salling-Mortensen's office.

nse University Centre, designed by professor Knud Holscher, Krohn & Hartvig Rasmus-
 firm of architects.

The Vollsmose project, housing area, Odense.

The building development Sct. Klemensparken, Odense. Architects A. and E. Eriksen.

Opposite: Odense Hospital. Architects K. Boeck-Hansen and Jørgen Stærmose. ▶

The Rosengård School in Odense. Architects Vagn O. Kyed and Per Kyed A/S.

Odense's Customs House. Firm of architects Jacob Blegvad, Aalborg.

buildings, *Fraugdegaard* dated 1588, a moated double house, just like Egeskov, but with a brick facade from 1769 and heavily restored between 1882–83. The second is *Bramstrup,* a baroque building from 1689 in three wings partly on older foundations and with a half-timbered servants' wing, dating from the later Middle Ages or early Renaissance.

Oregaard is a small half-timbered manor on North Funen west of Bogense. It consists of a single building with high, very heavy stone foundations from the beginning of the 16th century and on this is a building of tight-packed timber work a storey high, dating from the 1580s. This manor has also undergone extensive restoration.

Hollufgaard, that lies within the limits of the city of Odense, has preserved a two storey high building without wings, but with three ponderous towers looking onto the courtyard. The house, which was built in 1577, had two turrets and two bays looking onto the garden, as well as having sweeping gables.

The Italian, master Dominicus Baetiaz, has enriched many manor houses on Funen with a southern strain of the Renaissance inspiring his work. He was a very capable mason and avoided minutiae in sandstone whenever possible. His major work, the sumptuous and superb *Holckenhavn* near Nyborg, built without sandstone, has rich and elaborate decorations made of pure brickwork.

Holckenhavn, the first phase of which was finished in 1585, consists of a north and an east wing. When the construction continued in 1631–34 Baetiaz's gate-tower was reconstructed and the west wing with a chapel, as well as the south wing in which the gate-tower is found, were constructed. The walls built by Master Dominicus had ashlar masonry in which the narrow, polished band creates a rich effect of a relief. On top there are meandering patterns made in the same way. The large, white-washed portal is an excellent example of what actually can be done with bricks.

The white *Skovsbo* near Rynkeby was built between

1572–79 and has sweeping gables, but is not in the same class as Dominicus Baetiaz. It has a stair-tower and two wings, one of which is of a more recent date. Skovsbo is remarkable by being Funen's most famous, or rather notorious, haunted house. It is deceased members of the Hardenborg family who both night and day play tricks on the place, and Skovsbo's luck depends on the fact that a Renaissance crucifix that stands near the road at some distance from the manor is always well maintained.

Gyldensteen near Bogense and *Ulriksholm* near Kertinge cove are of pure Renaissance design. Gyldensteen has ashlar masonry and sweeping gables on top, is surrounded by broad ramparts and has side wings which are partly baroque, partly classical. Altogether it is a stately and magnificent manor house built on land reclaimed from the sea.

Ulriksholm, which is greatly reconstructed, was built in 1646 by Christian IV. It has tall stair-towers topped by spires and is also surrounded by broad ramparts.

Wedellsborg north of Assens lacks the regularity of baroque, but its character is completely baroque. It is a house of the late gothic period that is somewhat rebuilt on the exterior, to which other wings have been added later.

A very distinctive building is *Glorup,* south-west of Nyborg, and originally a four-winged Renaissance castle, but reconstructed to baroque by Philip de Lange in 1743–44. The towers disappeared and a floor was taken off the wings. In 1765 a new reconstruction took place, this time by Nicolas-Henri Jardin and Christian J. Zuber, and the castle to a certain extent was given a classical look. The elegant temple-shaped ridge turret on the gate leaf was one of the additions from this time. The baroque character was, however, partly preserved and today Glorup is amongst our most distinguished buildings. The castle is surrounded by a very large beautiful park in the English style with a pond and a "Tuscan" garden temple with the statue of Andromeda by the sculptor Johannes Wiedewelt. The park is on the whole rich in garden figures and sculptures.

Hvidkilde, the large manor near Svendborg, has been altered to rococo style, whereas the small manor *Margaard* at Søndersø was built in this style and is considered one of the country's best rococo buildings. *Langesø* at Morud has both baroque and classical styles and the distinguished reddish-yellow house lies in the middle of a magnificent English park.

Krengerup in West Funen, where the whole of the large home farm is preserved, is also very distinguished and sterling. The finest classical house of them all on Funen is *Hagenskov Castle* just south of Assens. G. E. Rosenberg was the architect and again here the old home farm is intact. The rigid orientation of the central axis has been followed scrupulously. The white house lies at a dignified distance from the farm; the base and window casings are yellow, the walls are otherwise white and the beautiful pediment has a copper roof. The hipped roof has otherwise glazed black tiles.

On Langeland, the old castle, *Tranekær* lies high on its hill and is surrounded by a large park. The North wing was probably built in the 1200s and has enormously heavy walls of granite and brick. The west wing is also medieval and traces of a watchman's gallery above have been found. There were originally four wings, but in 1772, two of them were pulled down. During restoration in 1862–63 the buildings were given a strongly new gothic look and at the same time, the corner-tower was built. Under extensive restoration and examinations in the course of recent years, much of the building's original character has been exposed. Below the castle hill lies the riding ground and beside it, the theatre which is a beautiful baroque building with a mansard roof. The manor's stables were built about 1800. Tranekær was in the Middle Ages and the Renaissance one of Denmark's most significant castles and to this day the walls are scarred by the many encounters to which it has been subjected.

Valdemar's Castle on Tåsinge was built by Christian IV

in 1644, but since then it has been rebuilt in the baroque style and is amongst the best in the country. From the main building down to the sea are two precisely similar farm wings which flank a pond with a little island in the middle. At the end, the complex is completed by an elegant tea pavilion. At the junction between the house and the farm buildings there is on each side of the courtyard a gate leaf with red painted ridge turrets. The whole magnificent complex was constructed in 1754 with G. D. Tschierscke as the architect.

There are many other manors on Funen, amongst them many which indeed are worth seeing and which it was tempting to write about but in an introduction as short as this, it is not possible to include more than those already mentioned. It must just be hoped that the Danes are aware of their responsibility so that these places will be preserved for all time and so that there will always be something beautiful for tourists to experience when they visit our island.

Modern Building

by Ebbe Lehn Petersen

The building activity of more recent and modern times on Funen is not any different from that in the rest of Denmark.It must however be said that the number of projects and also often their size are substantially less than in the Copenhagen area.

International influences have naturally left their mark on Danish architecture and in the latter half of the previous century inspiration was largely sought from historical styles. The older part of Odense townhall, built in 1881–83, and designed by the architects J. D. Herholdt and C. Lendorf, is, for instance, greatly inspired by the townhall of Siena and appears in North Italian gothic style. (During a later, and generally successful, expansion of the building, designed by the architect B. Helweg-Møller and completed in 1955, the 45 metre high tower and the two side wings had to be demolished, thus weakening the imposing effect). The building of Copenhagen's townhall in 1892–1902 created a nationalistic feeling with impulses from ancient Scandinavian architecture as well as a fine sense of the textural effect.

The Danish village church was the main theme when Fredens Church was built in Odense in 1916–20, designed by P. V. Jensen Klint. It is a more sterling building than Jensen Klint's *magnum opus:* Grundtvig's Church in Copenhagen, where the village church is transposed into the size of a cathedral. The less ambitious building in Odense fits in better with the original model.

The nationalistic influence that was an attempt to adapt freely the local historical styles, was followed surprisingly by a cultivation of antiquity and neo-classicism around 1800. It expressed an endeavour to achieve a great and

69

pure architectural style, which was seen in the buildings by C. F. Hansen (Copenhagen's Cathedral and Law Courts), but with a greater interest placed on the material effect and stress on the workmanship.

The major example of this neo-classicism, and in addition a gem of Danish architecture, is Faaborg Museum, built 1912–15, and designed by Professor Carl Petersen. In the small country town it appears as both a modest and imposing building and internally it is a very opulent one. Dark rooms lead onto light rooms, side lights onto overhead lighting. The variations in the individual rooms' shapes, colours and the patterns of the mosaic floors help to give this small museum its own charm and make it an experience to walk in it.

At the conclusion of the 1920s the cultivation of historical styles eventually ended – neo-classicism ended with formalism. It was realized that imitating styles was not suitable for the large, modern assignments that a highly developed, technological era demanded. The architectural effects were simplified to more rational planning and a degree of standardization.

The old Danish tradition was studied again, not to copy it, but to learn a natural approach to the assignments. But only after the 1930s did international functionalism assert itself, inspired by the artistic association Bauhaus in Germany and the architect Le Corbusier in France. Harmony between form, construction and context was not unknown in Danish construction tradition. The traditional building material, brick, practically remained supreme, as brick buildings could precisely express the concept of functionalism, when freed from elements of historical style. It was possible to create an up-to-date and natural architectural style with this traditional material. The Public Library in Nyborg built in 1938–40, designed by the architects Flemming Lassen and Erik Møller, Copenhagen, is a very fine example of this »traditional« functionalism. In the area between Nyborg Castle and the Square was an old residence of a commandant which was demolished to give a better view of the castle from the square. There are canals around the area and in working out the details attention has been paid to this unique position. The building, which is a single storey, is divided into two wings, a larger and a smaller one which follow the canals on both sides. The north gable of the larger wing lies level with the terraced houses of the square and the smaller wing runs parallel with the castle. The contents of the building can be sensed from the exterior: the large wing contains the lending library, while the smaller one contains smaller rooms, offices, etc.

After the isolation during the Second World War there was a very strong desire to find inspiration from the outside world. Architects began to go on pilgrimage to the internationally famous architects' great works and learned about new methods of production and materials. Although some postwar Danish buildings are internationally famous, it is more the quality as a whole than individual examples that is the strength of Denmark's modern buildings.

From the middle of the 1950s industrialised building – montage building – begins to win the day. Prefabrication and standardization both of parts of the facade, doors, windows, but also of entire walls, became current at the expense of the traditional brickwork which however was never entirely abandoned. At the same time competitions encourage architects to find new solutions in presentation, materials and constructions.

After a competition the architects Jørgen Stærmose and K. Boeck-Hansen, Odense, were assigned the planning of Odense Hospital's extension, a project that is not yet completed. While the original hospital, according to the principles of the period, is built horizontally, with low, individual buildings, the nucleus of the new design is a high-rise building of 14 storeys with the wards, that rests on a broad two-storey building which contains the operating theatres and out-patient department. The new buildings are constructed in reinforced concrete with a facade of white concrete tiles with brown bricks as pillars between the windows.

When the modest hospital in Bogense was to be expanded from an area of 600 m² to 7,500 m² the architect, Salling-Mortensen, Århus, respected the modest, harmonic and unique look of the town. The expansion was divided into several, partly detached two-storey buildings which were further pressed down by the use of flat roofs. By adopting this principle one avoided in addition making the hospital look like an institution. Later the same firm of architects, following the same principles, was responsible for the building of a nursing home closely connected with the hospital.

Another nursing home – Provstegårdshjemmet – in Odense, planned by the architects A. and E. Eriksen, Odense, is completely built on one floor. The sense of an institution is obscured by placing green courtyards between the individual wings, by putting seats in connection with the passageways and by the choice of materials.

The Department for State Hospitals (Mental Hospitals) built in 1975–77 a state hospital for the mentally disordered on a site behind Odense Hospital. The building is designed by the architect firm C. F. Møller's Architect's Office, Århus. Before it was finished the regional council of Funen took over all psychiatric treatment, so the five »pavilions« of the cottage hospital are now included as a part of Odense Hospital's psychiatric departments. Only two of the pavilions are in actual fact wards, while the rest contain out-patient clinics, day hospital, etc. In the administration building of Haustrup's Factories in Odense the schematic division that normally characterizes modern offices is avoided and the building that is designed by Poul Kjærgård's Architect's Office in Copenhagen has been given a sculptural effect. The choice and treatment of the materials has also enhanced the building compared with the enormous production halls.

The shortage of buildings makes planning and construction of entire town districts necessary. The plan for Volls-mose is such a new housing area, growing up in the north-east outskirts of Odense. When completely developed the new area will consist of c. 5,000 buildings divided into different forms and with a great variety of types of flats. In addition all necessary functions for a town will be supplied – shopping centre, school, children's institutions, churches, hotel, nursing home and sports facilities.

The Vollsmose project is an attempt to create a new suburb with the same standards as a town and there is also an attempt made to systematically separate pedestrians from the traffic. A joint architects' office with Hans Jørgen Jensen, Oluf Rasmussen, Herman Ricka and Jørgen Stær-mose are behind the project and Samvirkende Bygge-selskab (The Federation of Building Societies) in Odense are the building owners.

Normally the newly built areas on the outskirts of most towns are individually built single family houses, often built by different building companies' standard designs, using prefabricated units. The parcelling out of the land is very traditional, with the aim of getting as many equally large plots as possible out of the available area and with the possibility of driving up to all the houses. Such newly built areas are not particularly uniform, but when gardens and other vegetation grow, it will lend some decoration to these areas.

In St Klemens in the southern outskirts of Odense the firm of architects A. and E. Eriksen have planned a building development consisting of terraced and linked houses. It is an attempt to plan a newly built zone so that it is not the vegetation that will endow it with the homogeneity it lacks, and to introduce differentiation of traffic, to allow pedestrians to walk in safety.

Newly built zones will need new schools, so a group of architects created the Central Office for Practising Architects on Funen and developed a building system by which a great number of schools are being built. Rosengård

73

school, planned by the architects Vagn O. Kyed and Per Kyed, Ltd., Odense, is an example of such a school in a newly built neighbourhood in the south-east outskirts of Odense. The further education of adults makes it necessary to build course centres, which are often placed on the outskirts of larger towns in picturesque surroundings. The Svendborg School Course Centre was built by the Semi-skilled Workers' Association in Denmark and put into use in 1977. The aim of the school is to provide the setting for specialist courses for the association's members and there is room for 60 students and 10 instructors. The school is built in what was previously an orchard east of Svendborg and the area of the school includes a public park with beautiful scenery. The school building has a low, elongated plan that follows the form of the terrain and therefore underlines the landscape's character. The building is constructed in mocha-coloured brick with horizontal light-coloured bands of concrete and the roof surface is covered with yellow tiles. The project was led by the architect Oluf Rasmussen, Odense.

In 1964 permission was given to build a centre for higher education and research in Odense and in 1966 a public architects' competition was held. The winner was the firm of architects Krohn and Hartvig Rasmussen, Copenhagen, and since 1971 Odense University Centre has been built in the wooded part in the large area south-east of Odense which is reserved for the university. The buildings appear to be relatively low, consisting of a cellar and one high and two low storeys in the same section. The construction is made of pillars, girders, floor and roof sheets of reinforced concrete, cast on the spot. The facades are of lightweight, self-supporting units built on to a steel framework and covered with Cor-Ten steel sheets externally, while internally the covering is partly of painted steel sheets and partly plasterboard.

Town renovation with the construction of individual houses in a street makes special demands in order to produce successful results. A certain conformity with the proportions and height of the surrounding houses is essential. When building owners who are financially well endowed buy up a row of houses or an entire block and build large new constructions that do not take account of the neighbouring houses, then things can go very wrong indeed.

Kay Boeck-Hansen, Odense, designed a building for Kjøbenhavns Handelsbank in Vestergade in Odense, which was built in 1958. The building consists of a front building on to the street in five floors and an extension of one floor on to the courtyard which contains the actual bank building. The compact building, which is constructed in reinforced concrete with a facade of Norwegian marble, is, along with Magasin's (a department store) two adjoining buildings, a good example of town renovation.

Many towns in the last 15 years have undergone such great changes that they have almost lost their character. Political and town-planning intervention to solve traffic problems has often been the cause, and a lack of any sense of preserving and rehabilitating old houses has made the decisions easier, so that even houses that were listed were torn down. Nørrebro in Odense was a complete neighbourhood of small dwelling houses from the previous century which, in connection with the penetration of a large road, was seriously reduced and finally totally destroyed to make room for large new public buildings. In 1977 Odense's Customs house, designed by Jacob Blegvad Architect's Office Ltd., Ålborg, was built here, according to a specially developed office system. The system is a framework construction of prefabricated reinforced concrete units with light-weight facade units, externally covered with black Eternit sheets. The external concrete remains untreated and the roofs are covered with red tiles – it is therefore purely an office block, without the distinguished exterior of the previous Customs house.

It has been possible by legislation during the past dozen

years or so to receive financial help for the extra expense incurred by preservative reconstruction of houses or entire areas. The townpeople's wish to preserve their town as unchanged as possible and the increasing interest in old buildings will make it difficult in the future to put roads through the town and set up parking places. During 1970–75 Odense Municipality carried out a programme of preservative reconstruction in the area around the Hans Christian Andersen Museum – this is the final remains of an old market town settlement. Behind the old facades modern buildings have been installed, which makes the salvaging of the houses possible and thus preserves the architecture of a lost era. The project is carried out by the architects Knud, Erik and Ebbe Lehn Petersen, Odense. In Lotze's Garden, so greatly reduced by the motorway, Thomas B. Thrige's Road, and behind the reconstructed houses, there has been an extension of the Hans Christian Andersen Museum by the same architects, and to conclude the reconstruction of the neighbourhood the museum buildings, built in 1930, have been completely converted, except for the large domed hall. By the proportioning of the new buildings and by the choice of materials they have tried to respect the old market town settlement.

The History of Funen

by Anne Okkels Olsen and Bente Rosenbeck

Antiquity (until A.D. 800)

Funen lies in the middle of Denmark. This situation has played a significant role in its history. Jutland has had to deal with the storms from its southern border, while to the east it was Skåne and Zealand with Copenhagen that was the target. On the surface it may appear as if the island's geographical situation in Denmark has resulted in a total lack of history. But in many respects Funen is a special case.

Throughout Denmark's *antiquity* the island was indeed inhabited, but not very densely, especially if one considers the good soil. The people survived by hunting, supplemented by fishing and gathering shellfish. The refuse from these Stone Age settlements is still found in kitchen middens, and remains of this culture are still in evidence around the coast of Funen: a large shell heap, a genuine kitchen midden has been excavated on Langø island and smaller settlements are known on, amongst other places, Hindsholm and Fyns Hoved.

The greatest revolution in Danish history is the transition from *hunter/food-gatherer culture to agriculture,* which happened 4,000 years ago. It was a question of a gradual development by which man began by taming animals and cultivating plants. Agriculture brought about two fundamental changes: first that man was able to survive when settled in one place, secondly that the same area of country could provide food for a good deal more people. A *village community* could be formed.

One of the great eras of Funen's history was in the *Later Stone Age* (2700–2000). Between Odense and Bogense

77

there was a dense community of settled farmers with domestic animals. South Funen and the islands are to the foreground in this period. The monuments of this peasant culture are the many stone cists:

Graves built of boulders: cairns, that is mounds with a ring of stones and a square burial chamber of large side stones and a large roof stone, and passage graves, that is, a stone chamber with cover stones on top and with passage.

These graves are always only found in the coastal areas and especially on the islands, e.g., Langeland with Myrebjerg passage grave, King Humble's grave, Egelykkedyssen and Bjerreby passage graves. Near the Hindsholm village of Martofte is to be found the largest, best preserved passage grave on Funen, with a 7 metre long passage and 10 metre long chamber.

The construction of the many graves bears witness to a surplus and a stable society. Agriculture must have provided food in such rich quantities that there was surplus strength left to build graves instead of solely providing food. Peasant culture had made its entry and with it came a terrific change to man's way of life. Mankind began for the first time to be independent of nature by producing his own food. The basis for the Stone Age peasant's existence was the flintstone axe – both weapon and tool for felling trees.

The Bronze Age civilization (2000–500) we do not know very much about. The magnificent gold and bronze finds bear witness to the existence of an upper-class culture. Very many gold bowls, for example, have been found on Funen. Faded deposits and finds of votive offerings can be found in many places. Two lurs found in 1808 in a bog in Tellerup near Ørslev belong to the most exquisite of the bronze age finds on Funen. Judging from these finds, we can see that Funen must have had a large and prosperous population.

Cultivation of the land continued steadily throughout the Bronze Age. During the *Iron Age* (500 B.C. – A.D. 800) a more permanent agriculture developed with animal husbandry and cultivation of plants. An important prerequisite for this type of agriculture was iron. Whereas the raw materials for bronze (tin and copper) had to be imported, there are many signs that point to the fact that Denmark at an early time was self-sufficient in iron. This metal could be extracted from bog iron ore which was easily accessible in many places in Denmark. The metal was extracted and forged into proper tools such as axes, knives, sickles and in the later Iron Age to ploughshares. This wealth of implements can be seen in the Vimose find (near Odense). It is the country's largest bog find from the Later Roman Iron Age and contains c. 4,000 items: weapons, riding equipment, domestic utensils and tools, including harvesting implements, planes, forgers' implements, bits of wagons, etc. From the final period before the Viking Age (400–800) several rich finds of gold have been discovered, e.g., the Broholm treasure, which is Denmark's largest, weighing 4,5 kilos of gold.

The Viking Age

At the beginning of the Viking Age – around 800 A.D. – Denmark and Scandinavia represented a border region in relation to the rest of Western Europe. The Scandinavian region had not been under the Roman Empire and had not been organised in a real polity.

In the Viking Age the North flourished and reached its golden age. It was a period of political, economic and military expansion, greater than had ever happened before or was to occur later. A united state with church connected was created, which led to a cultural life corresponding to the rest of Europe's with the ability to write and the formation of towns. The central part of the country at that time was north and south Jutland, but also on Funen rapid development occurred.

Many of Denmark's distinguished Viking finds are here:

79

the *Ladby Ship,* the *Glavendrup Stone,* the garrison camp *Nonnebakken.* The town of Odense, like Århus, dates from the late Viking Age. It was the water that united all of Denmark, as the land was covered with impenetrable forest. The great changes that occurred in the Viking era were determined by the connection with the sea, by ships, sailing routes and changed trading routes. The Danes managed to control the trading routes between the Baltic and the North Sea (the traffic connection at the south of Jutland via the river Eider to Hedeby near the Schlei). In addition there was a trading route from the North through Russia to Arabia. It was slaves first and foremost that were traded with, but also hides and furs. Other functions than piracy, foraying and colonisation must be attributed to the Vikings. The key to an understanding of the Viking era is trade and the myth of the uncivilized Vikings that exists must be revised. Peaceful commercial intercourse was an important part of the expansion of the Norse. Likewise the Viking expeditions proceeded from a prosperous, expansive society and not from impoverished, overpopulated areas. The Vikings knew how to exploit the external trading conditions, i.e. the creation of trading routes from south to north Europe.

The reason for their ability to exploit these trading conditions must be found in their development of ship engineering. By the beginning of the Viking period even, the Scandinavians had developed excellent sailing ships. The use of the sail had increased the speed enormously, but in order not to be completely dependent on wind, the ships could still be rowed. One of these ships was found in 1935 on Funen in a Viking grave, the *Ladby Ship.* For many years this was Denmark's only Viking ship, decidedly more poorly preserved than the Norwegian ones, Gokstad, Tune and Oseberg. Most of the woodwork had rotted away and only the nails lay in position. The anchor, weapons and also the skeletons of some horses lay in the ship, which itself was 21.6 metres long and 2.85 metres broad with 16 pairs of oars. It was both narrower and lower than the well-known Norwegian ones and consequently archaeologists for a long time were uncertain as to its function. But late in the 1950s five ships were found in the Roskilde fjord which confirmed that the Ladby ship was a warship. The Danish ships were proportionately narrower and lower than the Norwegian ones, because the Danish were built for the flat beaches and not for the deep Norwegian fjords. The Ladby ship could have reached all round the Danish coast line, as it draws less than half a metre when fully manned. With four horses on board the ship could sail up to the beach with its broadside facing the land, so the horses could literally spring right onto dry land.

The ships became the symbol of the Vikings and also represented the zenith of their technical knowledge and ability. Their enemies hated and envied them these ships, while the Vikings considered them a means of power, their dearest possession and follower in death.

The cultic significance of the ship can be seen, e.g., in the stone ship at *Glavendrup* in North Funen. A ship structure that must have been 60 metres long and 12 metres broad. The large, upright monoliths are so placed that they form the outline of a longship, a substitution for a real ship such as at Ladby. A chieftain's grave without chieftain, but with an informative runic stone in the bows. This runic stone with its 110 characters contains the longest inscription in Denmark, and with this inscription Funen emerges out of the anonymous state of not having written records.

Town Civilization came to Denmark in the Viking period. Towns grew up around tradingposts and places of worship. What distinguishes a town from a country village is the fact that the inhabitants of a town largely consist of tradesmen and merchants, for whom agriculture is of secondary importance and they survive by selling their wares.

The first towns developed because of international trade and its need of protected market places: Schleswig/Hedeby and Ribe (700). Towns such as Odense/Århus composed the next step in the formation of towns, connected with the fact that local trade also started along the country roads. Odense is mentioned as an episcopal residence in a charter issued by the German King Otto III in 988. Archaeological exploration of the town has not come very far, but it should be remembered that near the oldest Odense the king – either Harald Blue-Tooth or Svend Forkbeard – built the Viking fortress Nonnebakken. The form of the name on coin inscriptions "Odin's Temple" points to a basis in a place of worship, but no finds to date suggest an older foundation for the town than the end of the 900s.

Nonnebakken is one of the four circular fortresses that go under the name of "Trælleborg" and which must be assigned to a date around 1000. Nonnebakken is the site that has been investigated least, because of its situation in the middle of the city of Odense. The fortresses are all constructed according to the same pattern, but differ in size. The construction bears witness to a brilliant technical knowledge and effective organisation by virtue of their uniformity and geometric precision. They show that the royal power was strong and well organised. The fortresses we know probably had room for c. 6,000 men and a fleet of about 80–100 large ships. The general opinion for a long time has been that they served as training camps for soldiers in connection with expeditions to England. In Svend Forkbeard's era Viking expeditions to England were reintroduced on a large scale, and the conquest of England completed in the reign of his son, Canute. Under him a North Sea empire including Denmark, England and possibly Norway and Sweden was built up. This empire dissolved immediately after the death of Canute (1035), which led to a decisive and permanent weakening of Denmark's position. The fortresses were therefore in use only for a short period but perhaps they had another function. They have strong defence works which must point to the fact that they clearly mistrusted the surrounding population. They can very well have been "punitive" fortresses

Funen does not only have small town communities but also sheltered inlets and beaches where the sound of birds, the smells, the blue and gray spring skies and the beat of the surf cannot have changed much in the past few thousand years.

that served to preserve the royal power over a recalcitrant people. The king's power was being strongly established in this period and the same was the case with the Danish church, especially in the second half of the 12th century when Odense became a bishopric and many churches were built on Funen. At this time we enter a period of peaceful development in which king and church began to cooperate.

This did not last, however. Trouble grew up in the time of the sons of Svend (1074–1134) who struggled for power. *Canute* (1080–1086), called St Canute, played an important role in the island. There have been two opposing views of Canute, one being the very pious conqueror and the other the tyrant. We know very little about his internal government but there is a degree of agreement that his actions elicited a dissatisfaction amongst the people that led to rebellion and ended with his death. The conflict is thought to have concerned ecclesiastical reform and the king's right to all property that was not possessed by any-one else. Both these point to the fact that Canute was an advocate for a new and stronger power with greater influence on the church, the administration of justice and warfare. However uncertain we are about what created the conflict between Canute and his people, we know that it ended in open insurrection. A rebellion broke out in Vendsyssel, and Canute had to flee through Jutland to Odense, where he confined himself in the royal court. After that he had to seek refuge in St Alban's church where he was killed in 1086 along with his brother, Benedikt, and 17 retainers. The following years Denmark was struck by crop failure. Such a catastrophe had to have an explanation and the most obvious one was to regard it as divine punishment for the murder of King Canute. The clerics in Odense were quick to seek Canute's recognition as a holy martyr. There were "miracles" at the grave of the king which were taken as acknowledgement of sanctification. His holy bones were buried after that in a stone sarcophagus which was removed to the crypt in the new, as yet incompleted, stone church which King Canute had begun. In 1101 the dead king was canonized by the pope and the occasion was celebrated with a great church festival in Odense on 19th April, during which the deceased tyrant, now called "Saint" was buried with ceremony in a shrine. The shrine still stands today in the crypt under St Knud's church. The canonization of Canute implied success for Odense. Erik Ejegod, the king's brother, invited a community of monks from an English Benedictine monastery whose special job it was to attend to the cult of his brother in the monastery that was dedicated to St Canute and which later was to serve as Odense church's chapter-house. Both the church and the monastery in later periods had great royal privileges conferred on them. In return the cult of Canute helped strengthen the kings' power as it sanctified the Danish kings.

Attached to the cult of the royal saint Canute is the so-called Odense Literature, one of the first Danish texts of a historical nature. An English born priest Ælnoth around 1120 wrote his Latin biography of the royal saint in St Knud's monastery. In this way Odense became a centre for literary culture around 1100.

The Middle Ages

While the Viking period marks an almost unbroken period of progress, the Middle Ages includes both progress and regression. The increase in building which featured strongly in the Viking period, continued until around 1300. The population increased, the cultivated area expanded and agriculture was made effective. It is in this period after the year 1000 that the many villages on Funen were established. In order to get food for a growing population significant areas of ground were cultivated. An important element in this development was partly the wheel plough, partly the improvement in yield by using the three-course system. Compared with the Viking period there was a concentration around the large estates. The leading powers, the king and the church, came to own complete and partial villages. The slave production of the Viking period was therefore not completely replaced by independent peasants. Copyhold farms were common. The number of peasants who themselves owned ground became less in the course of the Middle Ages. More and more gave themselves over to a great land owner. We therefore had a type of Danish feudalism.

The progress was halted around 1300 when a crisis occurred. The copyholders' situation deteriorated *inter alia* because their land had been reduced. This forced a large number of the population under subsistence level and meant that in bad years and when crops failed the poor died in their thousands. Plague and other illnesses did not improve their situation. From 1300 the Danish people stagnated.

This was one of the dark sides of the Middle Ages. On

other fronts there was rapid development, for all the market towns on Funen originate in this period. *The establishment of market towns* received fresh stimulus from the military defence fortresses which were built in the time of Valdemar I in connection with the war over the Baltic. Relations with the German empire were not clarified and the Wends plundered the Danish coast from the south. Funen lay in the centre and Valdemar I set in operation a nation-wide defence plan. In this way the king combined his foreign policy with his building programme. Danish sovereignty over the Storebælt was ensured by the construction of a town and fort on the Funen side of the Storebælt, namely *Nyborg,* which according to tradition was founded in the 1170s by King Valdemar's nephew Knud Prislavsen, the son of a Wendish prince who had become a retainer of the king. At the same time there was a fort established also at Svendborg. The beginning of Valdemar's reign was peaceful; trade created towns which in consequence often lay at the head of a fjord or bay and therefore had an extensive hinterland as well as access to the sea. *Kerteminde* which first became a market town in 1413 was the export harbour most used by Odense merchants. Apart from Kerteminde the Odense merchants used *Assens* as an export harbour, especially for the export of bullocks. Assens sprang up in the 1200s and in the Middle Ages became important as a ferry station for Jutland. Thousands of oxen and live pigs were yearly shipped from Assens to Haderslev and from there southwards via Jutland. *Middelfart* provided another ferry station to Jutland but remained a modest size throughout the Middle Ages, supporting itself from the income from the ferry and fishing.

Bogense, on the other hand, expanded unlike Middelfart, until it became one of the most flourishing towns in North Funen, only surpassed by Odense. The town received its first privileges at the end of the 1200s; its main trade in addition to agriculture was the corn and beef trades.

Nyborg became what one might almost call the royal town of Funen. The Danehof, a national assembly of noblemen whose authority covered legislation and the administration of justice, was held here in the Middle Ages until 1413. The most epoch-making meeting at Nyborg Castle occurred in 1282 when Erik Klipping had to sign his coronation charter, whereby the royal government entered into political cooperation with the Danish aristocracy. The royal and ecclesiastical powers were supplemented by a third authority, the nobility.

Both *Fåborg* and *Svendborg* can be traced back to the 1200s. Svendborg in the Middle Ages was exposed to many attacks and was burned down once, during the various monarchs' controversies. The inhabitants of both Svendborg and Fåborg took a keen interest in trading with, *inter alia,* the Skåne market. Fåborg was politically and economically attached to the Dukes of Schleswig throughout the Middle Ages, in that the town belonged at times to the Danish king and at times to the Schleswig dukes. Fåborg reveals part of Funen's history on the national political front. The kings bestowed fief on nobles and others of position, as was the practice in Europe. The South Funen islands in particular with their limited area proved suitable for such endowments. Langeland and in particular Ærø were sometimes under the one, sometimes the other overlord.

The 1300s was Funen's darkest period politically. Because of the economic difficulties of the royal power, Funen was pledged to the Counts of Holstein in 1317. When Valdemar Atterdag became king in 1340 he began a systematic redemption of the Danish kingdom. Disagreements about the conditions and the sum of the mortgage created disturbances. The nobles in Jutland sided with the Counts of Holstein and this led to many disturbances. In 1357 the higher nobility of Jutland raised the standard and occupied Odense. Valdemar with his cavalry from Zealand succeeded in defeating the uprising and forcing them to make peace. After the peace treaty of 1358 the Counts of Holstein disappeared from Funen and a more peaceful period could begin.

Modern Times (1500–1800)

The growth of the market towns in the Middle Ages was only relative. In the 1500s by far the largest section of the population was still employed in agriculture. After the Reformation the ground was largely owned by the crown and nobility, divided almost equally between the two. The king and nobility were therefore the two decisive power factors in society and this period was noted for its power struggles between the two sides.

The villages constituted at the beginning of this period the major economic management unit. The manors were still quite small and the lords of the manors' land possessions were made of farms scattered here and there. But during the 16th and the first half of the 17th century the crown and nobility began to collect their possessions around their manor estates. The peasants owned only in very few cases the ground they cultivated. Most were copyholders, that is, they rented their ground from the lord of the manor in exchange for a tax, usually in the form of corn. This payment meant that in years of harvest failure because of weather, war or illness, it was difficult for the Danish peasant to stay alive. In addition to the manorial dues the peasant was obliged to do tenant work on land other than that he had leased. This latter obligation was drastically increased during the period, because the nobility could profit in this way from the growing demand for corn and cattle by a sharply increasing state of prosperity.

Although the Danish farmer's life was first and foremost linked to the lord of the manor and agriculture, the farmers had a certain contact with the world outside the village by way of the market towns. The commercial life of the mar-

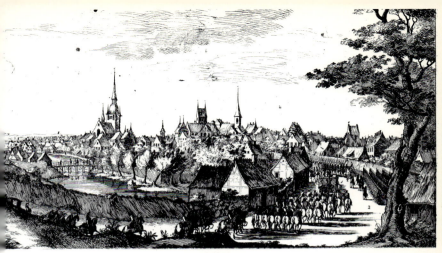

ense's days as the seat of Rigsråd meetings and supreme court were over with the centralised
of absolutism. Royal visits became less frequent and as time went by the nobility also opted
the court life of the capital city. However, Frederik IV who loved travelling, visited Odense,
lid Frederik V. In this picture can be seen the arrival of the absolute ruler in 1747 at St
gen's Gate duly escorted by the city's garrison and civic guard.

expansion of the transport system resulted in the building of railway ferries. The first were
paddle-steamers "Korsør" and "Nyborg", introduced in 1883.

...nmark experienced the worst winter for a long time at the beginning of 1658; the channels ...e all ice-bound, and on 30th January 1658 Karl X Gustav marched with 12,000 men over ...ebælt to Funen. (Copperplate engraving by Erik Dahlberg).

The ship from the chieftain's grave at Ladby near Kerteminde immediately after the excavat in 1935. (*Nationalmuseet*).

ket towns depended originally on import from abroad, but in the 16th and 17th centuries export became more significant. In particular there were corn and cattle to export. This rearrangement strengthened the Danish trading situation to the cost of the German merchants who were previously so dominant. Danish commoners often received help from the king who considered an independent Danish economic life an insurance against the north German commercial cities' economic and political intervention in Danish affairs. Many Danish kings therefore supported the market towns in their demand for a monopoly on all foreign trading. At the same time the Danish royal power hoped meanwhile to weaken the power of the nobility which in the course of the 16th and 17th centuries had been significantly increased.

The "Count's Controversy" (the Danish Civil War, 1534–36) is *inter alia* a result of these clashes of interests. It is Denmark's last civil war and can be seen as a war of commons against the privileged nobility. Town people and farmers found support in Lübeck, that had democratised its government and would now like to have the captive Christian II reinstalled as part of the plans to create a new trade empire. A contributory reason for Christian II's capture was his legislature concerning market towns, by which he had tried to strengthen the merchants and thereby weaken the nobility. It was also the nobility that caused the king in 1523 to leave Denmark under compulsion.

Having hesitated for a while, the nobility gathered its forces against the town people and farmers, seeking support from Christian III. Late in May 1534 mercenaries from Lübeck under the leadership of Count Kristoffer of Oldenburg (hence the name: the Count's Controversy) carried out an attack, first in Holstein and shortly after on Zealand, where he was received by town people and farmers as a liberator and acclaimed as Christian II's deputy.

The uprising was not long in coming to Funen. After the swift success on Zealand the first envoys of the Count were sent to Svendborg to incite the town to rebellion; this was easily done, as Svendborg had already been the first market town on Funen to take the side of Christian II. In the middle of July a group of insurgents marched on the castle of Ørkild, owned by the Bishop of Odense, Knud Gyldenstierne, one of the many forces behind the capture of Christian II. The castle was apparently taken by surprise and the buildings burned down. The same fate befell the town of Ørkild. From here the insurgents set off for Odense and on the way their number grew as many farmers and most market towns except Nyborg joined the rebellion. On the way to Odense many manors were taken and many ransacked or burnt down. When they arrived in Odense the rebels captured Knud Gyldenstierne's bishop's palace which was situated where the present home for unmarried ladies of rank now stands. The castle on Næsbyhoved was also plundered and burnt down, but after that the rebellion as a collective movement seems to have dispersed.

Meanwhile the newly elected Christian III gathered a force in order to relieve Funen. It consisted largely of country lads from Holstein who were landed on Funen late in July and in conjunction with the existing troops of the nobility organised the destruction of the rebels, so that all of North Funen would fall into the king's hands. Odense was captured by storm and when the situation on Funen seemed to have been stabilized, the king's troops were withdrawn to Nyborg.

In the month of August Count Kristoffer landed his reinforcements near Kerteminde and advanced towards Odense and Svendborg where the townspeople acclaimed him in the name of Christian II, just as had occurred in Skåne and Zealand. However, Nyborg castle had to be approached with cunning. The count's troops managed to sneak into the town and cut off the Castle's water supply, so that the moats were emptied, thereafter Nyborg eventually came into rebel hands. During the battle over Nyborg Castle the whole of the northern part of the town as well as the old St Helge Church completely burned down.

With the fall of this strongpoint the king's troops and those from Holstein were driven back over the Lillebælt and the entire island now was in the hands of the rebels and Lübeck. This situation lasted well into 1535, as Christian III had to suppress an extensive peasant revolt in North and Central Jutland.

A certain night in March 1535 the king, however, landed storm troops at Helnæs, south of Assens. The leader was the royal general Johan Rantzau, known for his brutal suppression of the rebellion in Jutland. On 20th March Rantzau's troops met those of the Count at Favrskov Bjerge, southwest of Årup, defeated them and pursued them to Assens which was besieged, while the rest of Funen was quickly recaptured after brutal slaughter. In April Lübeck sent reinforcements to Funen to help the rebellion, Odense was captured back again and for a second time stormed – this time because the town had yielded to Christian III too quickly. Otherwise both sides had to be content with preparing for the decisive battle.

On 11th June 1535 the battle was joined at Øksnebjerg. The count's troops suffered a decisive defeat. The besieged in Assens now recognized that the battle for Funen was lost. The troops went on board some ships from Lübeck and the town was abandoned to plundering, as was the custom. Fåborg, Svendborg and Odense were also plundered by Rantzau's troops.

Even though the fact that the nobility retained their privileges was detrimental to the growth of the market towns, the towns on Funen grew quickly after the afflictions of the war. The rise in prices in Europe, that concerned agricultural products, was an advantage for a country whose economy was based on agriculture.

The Development of trade in agricultural products was especially perceptible in Odense where important merchant families came into being in the period after the civil war, e.g., the Mule family who earned a fortune in the cattle and corn trade. These great merchants invested their fortunes in magnificent townhouses, as they were excluded from buying agricultural land, not being nobility. The merchants' profuse building in Odense can be viewed as a counterpart to the very extensive construction of manors in the same period. The wealthy of Odense did not only comprise important merchants, but also the nobility to an increasing extent. Many of them had townhouses because a part of the official events in which the nobility participated were transferred to Odense, e.g., the Parliament of Funen (Landsting). Many noblemen built their distinguished Renaissance houses in the town for this reason.

The favourable conditions for trade in Odense affected its export harbour, Kerteminde. There was a certain degree of stagnation in Middelfart and especially Bogense, which was undoubtedly caused by the fact that the merchants' most important source of income was the export of cattle, which was being exported from other harbours. Neither did Svendborg quite reach its previous stature. Thanks to its situation the town had struck up a substantial trade with Lübeck in the Middle Ages, but when this began to be ousted in the Baltic by the Dutch, the central point shifted north east. In spite of progress after the civil war the town never regained its leading position in the trade life of South Funen. The same was the case for Fåborg. Nyborg was the South Funen town that was best able to put the changed trading conditions in the Baltic area to its own advantage, and during the 16th century it rose to be one of Denmark's most important trading towns. Nyborg was also known for the extensive buildings erected by its wealthy merchants. Among these Mads Lercke's house in Slotsgade is still preserved. The town enjoyed the king's favour in as much as Christian III ensured that the burned part of the town was rebuilt and Nyborg Castle repaired and improved.

Slowly the boom period ebbed away and from the 1650s

onwards marketing problems began for agricultural products, a decline that was increased even more by the *Swedish Wars of 1657–60*. It was Denmark that declared war on Sweden in June 1657, because the Danish king, Frederik III, wanted revenge for the hard demands the Swedes had made in the Peace of Brømsebro in 1645. The Swedish king, Karl X Gustav, quickly reacted, however, and he was conqueror of all of Jutland as quickly as October. The conquest of Funen was postponed as the Danish fleet was superior to the Swedish one, but the very severe winter of 1657/58 deprived the Danes of this advantage. The ice between the channels froze solid and the Swedes could walk over to Funen. On January 30, 1658, the Swedes landed at Tybring Vig where the Danish defence army was quickly defeated and the next day the Swedes advanced on Nyborg which capitulated almost immediately. The Swedish king then wanted to advance on Zealand. Rather than march via Nyborg he decided to continue over the ice via Tåsinge, Langeland and Lolland. Soon after that the Swedish troops approached Copenhagen. The Danish government was seized by panic and could think of nothing but to seek peace at any cost. On 26th February peace was signed at Roskilde.

It did not take long, however, before the Swedish king broke his promise to clear his troops away from Denmark. Quite unexpectedly he broke the conditions of the peace treaty and landed with new supply troops at Korsør and advanced on Copenhagen. This time the lightning expedition did not succeed and the Swedish army had to arrange a regular besieging of the town.

There were still Swedish troops on Funen since the time they had landed there over the ice. These troops were not only meant to ensure the conquered area did not defect, but also to make sure that Funen's resources were effectively exploited, which the Swedish army did in a well-organised way, a unique thing for armies at that time; e.g., the Swedes stressed the importance of not destroying the means of production in the conquered land. Instead they developed means whereby one could drain the conquered area of all its yield.

In the beginning of October, 1659, there was a chance of relieving Funen. Denmark was no longer alone. The great powers such as England, Austria and Holland now became involved in order to force a peace so that the Baltic trade life could be stabilized. After many deliberations and negotiations an assault on Funen was decided on. 5,000 men from Brandenburg, Austria and Poland were to land at Snoghøj and at the same time the Dutch and Danish fleets in cooperation land 6,000 men at Kerteminde. The plan was a complete success and the two armies met at Odense and advanced on the Swedish army that was only half their size. The Swedes retreated to Nyborg and the decisive battle took place outside that town on 14th November. It was a complete success for the allies and the entire Swedish army had to recapitulate with only the commanders-in-chief escaping over the channel by boat. In this way Funen was at length freed from the two year long Swedish occupation. The losses on both sides were great during the decisive battle. The Swedes lost 3,000 men and the allies 1,500. The tree-covered mounds, including Svenskehøj at Juelsberg, where it is thought that the fallen were buried, can still be seen. At least it was the last time Funen was directly involved in war.

After the civil war the towns on Funen quickly overcame the poverty created by war, but the situation in 1660 was quite different from that in 1536 when war was followed by good times for production and marketing. In 1660 the situation was just the opposite. The Swedish troops had forced the country to give massive contributions and added to famine came an epidemic which the Polish troops had brought with them and which spread quickly to the Danish population. The disease spread to Funen in 1660 and, combined with a terrible plague that had attacked the islands slightly earlier, it meant that the death rate was high.

It is thought that the total loss of human life by these two epidemics was about 15% of the entire Danish population. Compared to this the loss of life as a direct consequence of the war was minimal.

The hard times can be seen reflected in Odense. The nobility disappeared little by little from the town and the lively traffic died down. Much of the trade was reduced to retail business with the hinterland. Odense's life was no longer influenced by the rich merchants and that meant once more that the building activity that had previously left its mark on the town now languished.

The hard times that Odense suffered also inevitably meant a decline for the export harbour Kerteminde, while Bogense was reduced to a village with less than 500 inhabitants. Middelfart was just as badly hit by the slump which was intensified by the construction of Frederiksodde on the Jutland side (later called Fredericia) which was a serious competitor. Assens's fate was the same. The great decrease in the cattle trade meant that shipping also declined. A visible result of the hard times was the dilapidated state of the town's large Renaissance houses, whose owners lacked the capital to maintain them.

1750–1850

Only towards the middle of the 18th century did agricultural prices begin to rise, the population of Europe increased, the production of precious metal rose and the wars also influenced the prices. Eventually the fact that England was increasingly less able to be self-sufficient also began to play an important role. England was becoming industrialised and began to import corn. In the course of time this became decisive for Denmark's existence, but already by that time it became clear that agriculture was lucrative. Production on the manor estates was improved and at the same time the major agricultural reforms were brought about: adscription and tenants' indefinite villeinage were abolished. Many copyhold farms were changed to freehold in the ensuing period and around 1814 about 60% of the farmers were independent.

Around 1830 the price of corn began to rise and this not only benefited agriculture but also the provincial merchants just as much. The fast growing trade in agricultural and other products provided the impetus for the creation of many manufactured goods, e.g., the production of soap, sugar, cloth and many spinning mills were established. The steady advance led to the fact that Odense overtook Ålborg and Helsingør and once more made itself the country's largest market town. An additional benefit was that navigational conditions up to the town were improved in 1793 with the excavation of a canal from the fjord at Stige, in past Næsbyhoved Slotsbanke to Odense. In the town itself a harbour with two quays was constructed during 1797–1804. Thus in 1804 the first large ship could sail up the canal which was over 8 km. long.

The new canal meant that the town of Kerteminde lost its most important source of income as a port of disembarkation and warehouse for Odense. By going over to fishery the town was slowly able, however, to recreate its economic growth. The other towns on Funen were also influenced by the growing prosperity that resulted from favourable times for trade in agricultural products. Assens alone never quite reached its earlier importance even though shipping also increased here, not least after the crude pier was replaced by a real harbour dock in 1822.

1850–1970

This was the period when progress really occurred again. At the end of last century Danish society experienced an enormous reorganisation, along the same lines as that occurring in other European societies.

Agriculture was still Denmark's unchallenged major industry, in as much as over half of the population lived off the soil. In Denmark there was an economic profit in agriculture and in trading with agricultural products. Denmark did indeed follow the west European process of industrialisation, but through a side door, one might say.

Around 1880 Danish agriculture was influenced by the fact that the export of corn had gone badly for many years. It was priced out of the market by cheaper overseas corn. Danish agriculture did however succeed in weathering the storm by shifting production from grain to animals. The shift to dairy products went in the same direction. Agriculture was changed radically and was based on animal husbandry, milk production and to a certain extent also sugar production.

Industry began to increase in the 1860s and was mostly based on domestic industry. The majority of these were connected with further processing of agricultural products. Odense became, e.g., an important export harbour for agricultural products and in the town many factories were established that processed agricultural products.

One of the prerequisites for the adjustment to agriculture was *the expansion of the transport system,* partly by expanding the road network but in particular by constructing *railways.* The Nyborg-Middelfart line opened in 1865, the Odense–Svendborg line in 1876, the Ringe–Fåborg line in 1882, the Nyborg–Svendborg line in 1897 and finally Fåborg and Svendborg were linked on one direct line in 1916.

Nyborg's major source of income was still the ferry service over the Storebælt. With the introduction of the first large steamship, Mercurius, the crossing could be reduced to one hour and 50 minutes. The crossing of the Lillebælt was similarly aided, but in particular after opening the Lillebælt bridge in 1935 when the connection between Funen and Jutland became easy and effortless.

The common factor for all the railways on Funen was that they all radiated out from Odense. Towards the turn of the century innumerable new businesses shot up and the population rocketed up from 14,000 in 1860 to around 40,000 in c. 1900; that is it tripled in only 40 years.

Politically the region's constituency was influenced by the farming group and therefore by the Venstre Party (Liberals), while Odense preserved its conservative character. After the formation of the Radikale Venstre Party (Social-Liberals) in Odense in 1905 this party captured part of the Funen constituency.

Religious Revivals have also influenced Funen. In the 1820s a strongly religious movement sprang up amongst the laiety in the Kerteminde area, a movement that spread from there over the entire island and which later came in contact with Grundtvig, and this Grundtvigian movement gathered an increasing influence in the following decades.

The industrialisation and growth in trade that was beginning also had social consequences for the urban population. Country workers trickled into the towns and a new group of workers arose. Even though the large farms in the country were being replaced by smaller, independent farms, the small landholders and farm workers made up by far the largest group in agriculture. The living conditions of both the farm and the urban workers were not the best. The cost of food alone for these groups was 60–90% of their income. Today the U.N. places the starvation level at 60%. There is therefore no doubt that a large proportion of the Danish population starved and that the infant mortality rate was high. An increase in the standard of living in the course of the 20th century brought the Danish population over the starvation level.

The working class became larger in keeping with the growth of industrialisation and in time also gained political influence. For a long period, though, Funen was the bastion of conservatism. Social Democracy gained a foothold in the region and its market towns at a rather late date. During the 1930s that party won the position of mayor in all the market towns on Funen except Kerteminde.

The major events in Danish foreign affairs included the

If one wants to make one's world larger, one must travel slowly and take up less room in it. One is reminded by the veteran train of the time when Funen had the largest number of private railways in Denmark.

defeat by Germany in 1864, the First World War, the reunification (of N. Schleswig) in 1920 and the Liberation of 1945. The entire period was influenced by the relationship with Germany with whom Denmark, because of its geographical position and its smallness, was obliged to follow a careful and benevolent political position.

At the outbreak of the First World War the Danish government managed to convince Germany of its benevolent neutrality and England accepted the situation. The towns of Funen were greatly troubled by the unrestricted submarine war that Germany had declared in 1917 and by the widespread minefields. The loss during the war was never completely compensated for. The era of the sailing ship was over now. The schooners from Funen could not compete with the large maritime nations' modern, power-driven ships and the limited resources did not permit the necessary modernisation. In spite of this there was an optimistic feeling during the first years after the war, e.g., Svendborg Shipyard was established in 1916, Odense harbour was enlarged in 1919–20, Odense Steel Shipyard was constructed in 1917 and Odense Worsted Spinning Mill in 1926.

In the Second World War Denmark was not successful in remaining out of the war. On 9th April 1940 the country was occupied by German troops, Funen included. The establishment of a resistance movement on Funen was as good as started in the course of 1943. Because of its size Odense became the centre of the movement; e.g., the resistance developed to a widespread general strike during which there was confrontation between Odense people and German soldiers. In the beginning the sporadic sabotage was largely of a demonstrative nature, but in the course of 1944 it was largely made effective, for example the North Funen railway sabotage started up and, *inter alia,* the central equipment for the security system in the main railway station in Odense was blown up, but there were also many other targets for the Funen resistance movement.

The Post-War period was a time of stability. Around 1960 Denmark changed from being an agricultural country to an industrialised one. Up to 1960 agriculture made up more than half the Danish export. Only at the end of the 1950s was the importance of agriculture to the Danish society reduced. The mechanisation of agriculture meant that its work force was halved from 1950–1970, so that it accounts now for no more than 10% of all employed.

From 1958 onwards industrialisation made significant strides forward. Lindø shipyard at Munkebo, among others, was established and more towns on Funen had iron foundries and other modern industrial works.

Recently industry and trade have been hit by a recession; Lindø shipyard has had to reduce its size and the region, like all others, is hit by unemployment.

Schools and Education

by Viggo Land and others

An Outline of the History of Schools on Funen

The school system on Funen has its roots in the medieval church schools which were established in connection with the larger churches and monasteries. Beside Vor Frue Kirke (Our Lady's Church) in Odense there can still be seen the old school building which is today used as a chapel. In the 18th century influential individuals took the initiative to facilitate the schooling of the common people. In the years 1721–30 King Frederik IV had 240 schools established on his "Ryttergodser", that is, the royal estates from which the cavalry was conscripted. These so-called "Rytter schools" were a milestone in the history of the commoners' schooling, and many of these old school buildings have been in use right up to today.

Ludvig Reventlow, who in 1777 became the owner of the Brahetrolleborg estate in South Funen, had philanthropic ideals; he ardently worked for the education of ordinary folk and in the schools he had built on his estate there was a method of education that in its quality, its free form and friendly attitude to children, was strongly opposed to the contemporary methods. The furnishings from one of these schools have been set up in the old village school building in the open air museum – the Funen Village – in Odense.

This and similar initiatives were the forerunner of the first real school law in Denmark: the School Regulations of 1814. As a witness to the foresight that characterized these laws, one might point to the fact that they were largely retained as a satisfactory framework for the primary school system for over 100 years until replaced in 1937 by a new primary school law.

The Education Pyramid 1977

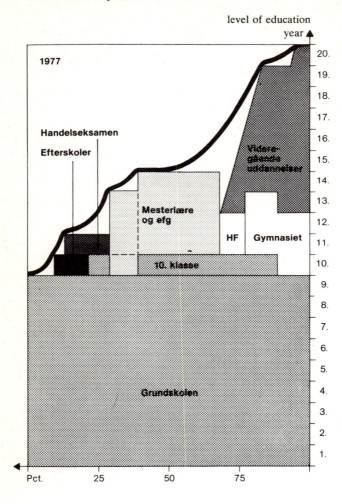

Source: Material supplied by the economic-statistic consultant to the Ministry of Education.

102

A particularly Danish view of upbringing and education grew up from the efforts of the Danish priest and inspirer of the people N. F. S. Grundtvig (1783–1872) and his views on popular education still influence the activities of the Danish school system. One of the first who put Grundtvig's thoughts into practice was the schoolmaster Christen Kold (1816–70). In the year 1851 in very primitive conditions, he had a high school built in Ryslinge in mid-Funen where he gathered farm servants for education. He later moved to Dalby near Kerteminde where he organised a free school for children and, contrary to the contemporary public children's schools, his initiative here was characterized by a deep understanding for the child and its potential. This school became the model for a number of so-called "Grundtvigian Free Schools", which were established in the following years, especially on Funen, but also all over the country. In 1862 Kold moved his high school to Dalum near Odense and this school is Dalum Agricultural School today.

The Danish Educational System

The Education Pyramid

The education pyramid will illustrate the distribution of those undergoing education in Denmark in 1977.

Grundskolen (the primary school) covers the 9 obligatory years of schooling. In the 10th year there are several possibilities: pupils can continue in the primary school's 10th form or go to a 3 year *gymnasium* (upper secondary school) or to the *grundlæggende erhvervsuddannelser* (basic trade and commercial education) in technical schools or commercial colleges (apprenticeship: *Mesterlære* or basic vocational training: *efg*). *Højere Forberedelseskursus* (higher preparatory course) – HF – is a 2 year programme, akin to the gymnasium, with a final exam largely of the same value as a "studentereksamen" (General Certificate of Education).

De frie efterskoler (free continuation school) is, along with the *Folkehøjskole* (folk high school) a private form of schooling that offers alternatives to the above-mentioned schools. They are supported by state grants of a substantial size.

In the diagram "Handelseksamen" (Commercial diploma) has been replaced since 1978 by the "erhvervsfaglig grunduddannelse" (Basic vocational training).

Folkeskolen (Primary and Lower Secondary School)

The form and structure of the primary and lower secondary school has been a central point in the postwar debate on education which the frequent law revisions of 1958, 1970 and 1975 bear witness to.

According to the 1975 School Act the primary school system includes a 1 year pre-school class, a 9 year primary school and a 1 year 10th class. A primary school structure has been attained in which the most important issues are the following:

1. That selection or streaming of pupils is avoided as much as possible in the actual children's schools. It is attempted to keep the children together in undivided classes and with the help of several supporting arrangements it is also attempted to keep the handicapped pupils integrated in ordinary classes.

2. That it is tried to encourage the individual pupil's all-round development by, *inter alia,* offers of a number of optional courses.

To a large extent the political debate has revolved around the question of the extent to which tests and examinations should be omitted or kept in the primary school. The result was a compromise: the Primary School may be terminated with an examination after the 9th class (the Primary School's Leaving Certificate – the same for all pupils) and after the 10th class by the Primary School's Further Leaving Certificate. In spite of the introduction of uniform examinations for all pupils, there was introduced split-level teaching (2 levels) in mathematics, physics/chemistry, German and English.

In the most recent developments in the primary school a noticeable tendency can be spotted to make the preservation of the smaller schools a reality, which are largely found in the country areas. But also in the market towns where for many years large schools have been built, there is a tendency in the direction of smaller schools with a maximum of 3 – 400 children. The tendency to decentralise is in keeping with the principles laid down for the reform of municipal legislation, which was introduced in 1970 and which has as a major issue the distribution of administrative duties to the local municipalities. The running of the primary schools is placed in the hands of the primary municipal authorities and a strong parent influence is ensured by the formation of parent-teacher associations in the individual schools.

Further School Education:
Gymnasiet and Højere Forberedelseskursus (Upper Secondary School and Higher Preparatory Course)

The *Gymnasiet* (Upper Secondary School) is a 3 year course and by far the majority of pupils come from the Primary School's 9th and 10th classes. Admission is on the condition that the previous school considers the pupil suitable for entry. In the first year the gymnasium is divided into a languages and a science side. From the second year onwards there are many optional courses, because the teaching is divided up into a number of branches. For the language pupils there is the choice between modern languages, classical languages, social studies or music studies, while the pupils in the science side can choose between mathematics/physics, social studies and natural sciences.

The concluding examination at the gymnasium is the "studentereksamen", the General Certificate of Education, which qualifies one for university study, as well as a number of colleges.

Højere Forberedelseskursus (Higher Preparatory Course) is a 2 year educational programme that concludes with the "Højere Forberedelseseksamen" (Certificate of Higher Preparation) which to a certain extent can be compared to the General Certificate of Education both in content and standard. There are no precise admission requirements. Characteristic of HF is that teaching is given partly in obligatory joint subjects and partly in optional subjects.

On Funen there are 3 State Upper Secondary Schools (2 in Odense and 1 in Svendborg), all of which have Higher preparatory courses attached to them, and 5 Regional Upper Secondary Schools (in Odense, Middelfart, Ringe, Glamsbjerg and Nyborg). 4 of these also have HF teaching. In addition Odense has a 2 year course which prepares for matriculation ("studenterkursus").

Trade and Commercial Education (by Helge Sindal)

The first technical schools and commercial colleges in the country were established after the middle of the last century by private initiative. About 100 years later the status of these schools was changed to independent institutions, for which the state took the economic responsibility for running.

For a time there were trade schools in a large number of towns, also in the smaller market and station towns, but today this training is limited to the larger towns, because of the greatly increased requirements for teachers' qualifications and equipment. On Funen there are now technical schools in Odense and Svendborg, while the earlier trade school in Ollerup is taken over by the State Teacher-Training in Commercial Pedagogy. Commercial colleges are found in Odense, Svendborg, Nyborg, and

Assens, while the commercial college in Fredericia also covers the north-west area of Funen, as the students have reasonably good access to the school on the Jutland side of the Belt (in Erritsø), because of the two Lillebælt bridges. The trade schools on Funen have altogether 12,000 pupils.

The present trade schools still offer the classical apprentice education during their master apprenticeship, but it is being replaced rapidly by the new basic vocational training – efg – by which pupils spend the first year after primary school in a trade school, before they go out to practical work.

Added to this there is a large number of further educational opportunities, both for full-time pupils and in the evening for adults who have been employed for some time. This is an area of education which is particularly systematized in the commercial colleges where further education leads on in a natural way to higher education such as that in the colleges of commerce, teacher-training colleges, universities, etc.

For day pupils the two most important streams in the commercial school are respectively the commercial high school (handelsgymnasium) and the computer science college (edb-skolen), both of which have a steadily growing entrance number. In the evenings there is the possibility for either a large number of single subject courses or for the so-called "merkonom" studies (commercial-economic), which for many have provided the foundations for further training for a career in business. The technical schools have established on top of this an equivalent further education programme which is called "teknonom"studies (technical-economic).

The semi-skilled workers' schools in Odense and Svendborg provide shorter courses in many technical subjects for the unskilled.

The Debate about Continued Education

During recent years there have been discussions in the field of education politics about the further development of education for the 16–19 year olds and in 1978 the Ministry of Education produced "U 90" – educational planning up to the 1990s, drawn up by the Central Committee on Education. The publication contains a number of reflections and suggestions for the further development of the Danish educational system and with respect to the 16–19 year olds' education it calls attention to the fact that it would be desirable to have greater co-ordination, so that the present very pronounced division between the choice of the more theoretical gymnasium which prepares for further study, and the more practical studies in trade schools is lessened. To promote such a development the teaching principles used in the Higher preparatory course (HF) and the Basic vocational training (efg) are found to be suitable.

Enkeltfagskursus (Single subject courses) is an educational opportunity which is particularly addressed to the slightly older pupils, who wish to supplement their education with examinations equivalent to the Primary School Leaving Certificate and Higher Preparatory Course (HF) Certificate. For many years these courses were placed under Leisure-time education, but from 1st August 1978 this type of education was placed under the control of the regional authorities by special legislation. As the name implies, it is normal that the pupil chooses single subjects in which it is possible to work with special areas of interest, and by putting together subjects over a number of semesters, a complete Higher preparatory course can be built up.

On Funen 10 large and smaller Single subject courses have been established, of which the largest with c. 4,000 pupils is in Odense.

Higher Education, Universities, etc.

by Helge Sindal

Denmark's oldest university, Copenhagen, is 500 years old. Århus has the next oldest which is only 50 years old. Today – 50 years later – the country has as many as six universities, but there is not much chance that more will be established for the time being.

In the period after the Second World War there was a growing interest in establishing university education in many areas of the country, and, as the third largest city, Odense came soon to be at the top of the list. The university of Funen was a reality in 1965 and in the first years it was situated in rented accommodation in the Odense Teknikum, but from the beginning of the 1970s there quickly began a comprehensive building programme for the university in the campus in the south-east part of the city.

Odense University has only the faculties of humanities, medicine and science, as well as a School of Business Studies (handelshøjskole) (commercial economy and commercial languages), which was transferred to the university from Tietgenskolen in 1978. There are c. 4,000 students.

Unlike a few of the older Danish universities Odense has not been strongly active politically. It has rather distinguished itself in purposeful work, not least in the area of research. At the same time it has made an effort to create close contacts with its surrounding society, first and foremost with the city of Odense.

In addition to the universities, there are on Funen a number of other institutions which offer further education. Odense Teknikum trains engineers who have already followed technical training.

The teacher training colleges in Odense and Skårup train teachers for primary schools.

The school for occupational and physiotherapists in Odense trains therapists for the social and health sector.

The Music Conservatory of Funen produces soloists in many different instruments and music teachers.

The Kindergarten and Leisure-time centre teacher-training college in Odense trains infant teachers for the social institutions for children and young people.

Leisure-time Education

As a point of interest it might be mentioned that the first Danish legislation on leisure-time education is contained in the School Regulations of 1814. The Regulations' § 28 reads: "For the young people who have been confirmed, but who nevertheless still wish to seek education, to practise further writing or arithmetic, or to take part in other useful education, there shall, after deliberation with the school commission, be held winter school twice a week. One hour for males in the evening and one hour for the girls in the day, all according to the school commission's closer consideration".

Leisure-time education, therefore, is based on a tradition that is now over 150 years old and along with the free organisation's work it has had invaluable significance for general education and thereby for the development of democracy.

In every Danish municipality, there is today an extremely wide range of educational offers in the area of leisure-time education for children, young people and adults in a range of freely chosen subjects and activities.

The law concerning leisure-time education is continually being revised in recent years and new educational offers are included under the law. The forms of the school from an administrative viewpoint are decided either by the municipalities or a special educational association, one of whose most important jobs is to see that the teaching is carried out according to this law. The two largest educational associations are AOF (the Workers' Educational Association) and FOF (the People's Educational Association). The municipal authorities and the state contribute economically with a substantial subsidy, thereafter the pupils themselves – in the case of adult education – contribute with a registration fee.

Ungdomsskolen (Continuation school) for 14–18 year olds offers a supplement to the Primary School's teaching and concentrates largely on subjects of a more recreative nature. For school-age children and young people under 18 *Interessegrupper* (Interest groups) are offered with subjects that come under the heading of hobbies. *Ungdomsklubber* (Youth clubs) are open to all young people between the ages of 14 and 18 and local authorities are obliged to provide accommodation for groups, clubs and associations that contain children and youths under 25. For adults the law on leisure-time education covers offers in *Aftenskoler* (Evening schools), *Aftenhøjskoler* (Advanced evening schools) where there is general further education, *Studiekredse* (Study groups), *Foredragsrækker* (Lecture series), and *Specialundervisning* (Special education) for handicapped adults. The *Folkeuniversiteter* (University extensions) are connected with the country's universities and teach knowledge of scholarly methods and results in courses and lectures.

The Libraries on Funen
by Carsten Tofte

In this section it is first and foremost public libraries as covered by the *Public Libraries' Act* that are referred to as the libraries on Funen. This legislation dates back to 1964 in its present form, although minor alterations here and there have been made without changing the fundamental direction of the basic law that covers public libraries and public school libraries. A revision of the act is being prepared with effect from 1980 at the earliest. In the state library system with free and direct access for all must be included the research libraries which, *inter alia,* are to be found on Funen.

Odense Technical Library was established in 1949 in cooperation with Odense Central Library. From 1949 the library has been transferred to Odense Teknikum. In addition to being the library for Odense Teknikum's students and teachers, it also serves the industries and technicians on Funen and is in addition open to the public.

Odense University Library was established in 1965 as an independent state institution under the Ministry for Cultural Affairs. Its major role is to serve Odense University and other institutions of higher and further education and research which are connected with the so-called Odense University Centre. The "Tietgenskole's Public Commercial Library" in Odense was incorporated into the university library in 1972. The Commercial Library began in 1961 in cooperation with Tietgenskolen and Odense Central Library. The university library's collections include Herlufsholm's School Library (founded 1565), Funen's Diocesan Library (founded in 1813 and administered by Odense Central Library from 1925) in addition to a number of larger and smaller private collections.

The Public Libraries' responsibilities are described in the preamble to the Act and read in the 1964 formulation as follows:

The purpose of public libraries is to promote the spread of knowledge, education and culture by making books and other suitable materials available free of charge.
(Public Libraries Act)

The libraries must consider the interests of all age groups and sectors of the population, and the different residential areas must be made equal as far as possible. In order to carry out this library service the act prescribes a system which is built up of independent municipal libraries; in principle a library in every municipality with one or more departments (branches) according to the population figure.

To take care of certain interconnected affairs every administrative region has a county library. For the region of

…tterskolen" (Cavalry School) in Hunderup which was previously a small village south of …nse, but which today is part of the city a mile or so from the city centre.

…ol conditions today are very different. Left: a glimpse of Mid-Funen's Gymnasium in Ringe. …t: The Regional Centre for Education Resources in Odense. It is a pedagogical workshop …h is at the disposal of teachers by producing teaching material.

Teaching in a pre-school class.

Rosengård School is the centre for the teaching of severely handicapped children in Odense. child in the foreground is learning to float without aids.
There are several classes in different schools on Funen in which severely handicapped chil are taught. To an increasing extent there is an attempt made to teach handicapped pupi normal classes.

new and – in the background – the old Little Belt Bridge between Funen and Jutland.

dsgavl Castle near Little Belt, built in 1784 in neo-classical style with a strong baroque ence and manor house design. Now it is a joint course centre for the Danish Norden ciation and the Mortgage Credit Association Denmark, the latter making this financially ible.
rleaf: Aerial view of Hindsgavl and its surroundings.

For many years Denmark has been called the country of the cyclist, and Funen is certainl
exception.

Many yachts and pleasure boats visit the Funen harbours in the summer, often anchoring sid
side with the fishing boats. Here at Lundeborg on East Funen.

ll Danish municipalities leisure-time education is offered such as evening school, evening
schools, study groups and special teaching for the handicapped.

**From the semi-skilled workers' school (*Specialarbejderskolen*) in Odense. Teaching in building trade.

Bogense Library. According to the Danish Library Law public libraries have been set up in municipalities.

Funen the library in Odense municipality also functions as the county library under the name of Odense Central Library. In addition there is a well developed tradition for cooperation between the different libraries; in some areas such cooperation is prescribed for them, but also when there is no provision in the law for it, there is a tradition for cooperation.

According to a recently completed analysis ("Fynske Folkebiblioteker", Odense Universitetsforlag 1978, ISBN 87–7492–242–4), 21 municipalities on January 1, 1980 have full-time library schemes with a qualified head librarian. 11 municipalities had part-time library schemes with non-specialist head librarians. The 32 municipalities on Funen make up a total of 30 administrative library "units". On Funen there are 30 main libraries and 109 branches with 139 permanent (stationary) libraries; in addition there are 8 library buses with 115 stopping places. The total number of places served by libraries is 254 in all.

Church Life

Christianity came to Denmark in 826 with the French Benedictine monk Ansgar, but it was not until 960 that the Danish King Harald Bluetooth described in runic script on the Jelling Stone at Vejle that "he made the Danes Christians". The Roman Catholic Church ruled until 1536 when the Lutheran church was introduced at the Reformation. During the following centuries the church was more and more pulled into the Autocratic system as a "state church" and only with the Constitution of June 5, 1849 the reorganisation of the church came about which forms the basis for the Danish Established Church, as we know it today.

At the same time as the Constitution ensured freedom of religion for the population, it also laid down that "the Lutheran church is the Danish Established Church and will be supported as such by the State". The Constitution also contained a paragraph that promises future legislation:

"The Established Church's constitution will be ordained by law". But in spite of the fact that c. 130 years have passed since then, a real Church Constitution has not been drawn up.

The Established Church (*Folkekirken*) is *not* a Free Church *neither* a State Church. The expression "Folke-kirke" (lit. = People's Church) implies that the church includes all people and is run by the people themselves. In practice it turns out that Parliament legislates over this area and the Minister for Ecclesiastical Affairs has the executive power, but the government avoids as far as possible any interference in "the Church's internal affairs".

The ecclesiastic administration may be illustrated by the following pyramid:

Monarch

Ministry for Ecclesiastical Affairs

Diocese	Bishop	Diocesan authorities
Deanery	Rural Dean	Deanery committee
Congregation	Priest	Parish council

The Established Church has for years undergone a process of liberalisation and by diverse laws the democracy within the church has been strengthened. The obligation whereby one is forced to use the services of the incumbent of a parish can be waived in favour of another priest, and the law of 1873 concerning the voluntary union of a certain number of members of the Established Church provides the opportunity for a group of people within the church to band together and form a congregation, choose their priest, build their own church or take over the parish church for their services.

The bishop of the Diocese of Funen lives in Odense, the diocese is divided into 12 deaneries and 254 parishes. A characteristic feature in the development of the parishes is the fact that while depopulation in the country districts has brought about amalgamations to a great extent, the de-

114

velopment of towns especially in Odense has made it necessary to build more churches and create new parishes.

About 95% of the Danish population are members of the Established Church but added to this are a large number of other faiths. In Odense there are independent churches for the Catholic congregation, the Baptists, Methodists, Adventists and Jehovah's Witnesses.

A particular feature in the life of a Danish congregation is the use of the rich treasure of hymns by three Danish hymn writers: Kingo (1634–1703), Brorson (1694–1764) and Grundtvig (1783–1872). Kingo has special connections with Funen in that he was the Bishop of Funen from 1677–1703. A memorial to him was erected in St Knud's churchyard.

Sport on Funen

by Knud Secher

Funen has and always has had during this entire century a rich and expanding sports life. The strongest and oldest roots in this tradition are the historical rifle and gymnastics associations that attract thousands of young people in Funen. A product of this movement is, amongst other things, the well-known Ollerup School of Physical Education, whose leader in the years between the wars, Niels Bukh, travelled around the world giving demonstrations with his gymnastic pupils, and because of that great respect was shown Danish gymnastics in many countries. In addition many marksmen from the Funen societies have distinguished themselves at international standards, e.g., in the Olympic Games.

A large number of private clubs and associations cultivate sport in the towns of Funen and receive economic help from the state and municipalities. The largest are naturally in Odense, where football and tennis predominate. Odense for many years has been called "Denmark's number one football town" and the clubs of Odense have won the Danish championship and the Danish Cup-Final many times. Tennis in recent years is no longer the elite sport for the few but is now a popular sport with many thousand participants and the same is the case with golf. Near Nyborg is one of Europe's finest golf courses where many foreign visitors also participate.

For many years Denmark has been called the country of the cyclist. Odense has one of Denmark's three well-known cycle tracks where the previous master in sprinting, Peder Pedersen, came from.

The Municipalities of Funen

by Hugo Mayntzhusen

The division of Funen into municipalities

Funen with its surrounding islands constitutes an administrative district, the *Region of Funen,* that has certain
superior functions, while the immediate municipal administration is in the hands of the 32 *municipalities* of the
region. These primary municipalities differ greatly in the
number of inhabitants, in that one of them (Odense) has c.
168,000 inhabitants, one (Svendborg) has c. 37,000, three
municipalities (Fåborg, Middelfart, Nyborg) have c. 18,000
inhabitants, while the remainder vary from c. 4,000 to c.
11,000 inhabitants.

The present division of municipalities dates back to 1970
when the *municipal reform* resulted in the amalgamation
and adjustment of the country's 25 regions down to 14
regions and c. 1,400 rural districts and boroughs to 276
primary municipalities. The reason for the municipal reform was because the existing division, which was largely
unchanged since c. 1840 and was in practice based on the
medieval ecclesiastical division into parishes, was felt to be
antiquated in many ways in relation to the population,
commercial and technical expansion.

The aim of the municipal reform, as far as *primary
municipalities* was concerned, was as follows:

i) A new division of municipalities around the towns
should be established, so that the population of one
town that found itself divided into a number of
municipalities, but which might be considered as in-
terdependent, would normally now be in one municipality. When boundaries were fixed the expected expansion of population and commerce should be consid-

117

ered, so that the town could have reasonable opportunities for expansion within the limits of the prospective municipality.

ii) With the amalgamation of the smaller municipalities larger and more manageable ones should be created that would not normally have less than 5–6,000 inhabitants.

With regards to *regions* two things happened:

i) "Market towns", that is boroughs that from ancient times have had certain special privileges, were excluded from the regional division, but in the future would be classified with the previous "rural districts" in the community of the region.

ii) The boundaries of the regions should be adjusted so that they followed as far as possible both the population and commercial contacts, and what was best fitting in respect to a suitable interpretation of the functions of the regions.

As far as Funen was concerned, the municipal reform resulted in three regions being reduced to one – the Region of Funen – while 73 rural districts and 11 boroughs were united to form 32 municipalities. As an example one might mention that the present Odense came into being by uniting the old Odense municipality with 12 surrounding municipalities.

One might ask to what extent there is satisfaction with the municipal reform. The answer is that the amalgamation of municipal administration into larger units with a professionally trained staff has been the necessary prerequisite to handle the explosively increasing demand for physical and economic planning and the still more complicated legislation. Undoubtedly the higher level of service enjoyed in the central municipalities has also spread to the usually less advanced country areas. On the other hand people do talk of the lack of contact between citizens and the elected representatives in the large municipalities, especially in recent years when the demand for "grass-roots democracy" has been to the fore. In this respect we should not forget the increased influence of the individual which is now developing, for example, in schools and child institutions, and also in sports clubs and semi-public organisations.

The organisation of the municipalities

The Danish Constitution since 1849 has contained a provision that the right of the municipalities to run their affairs independently under the supervision of the state, shall be secured by law. Concurrent with the municipal reform of 1970 a new law concerning the organisation of the municipalities came into effect, but it largely consisted of a harmonization of the rules that concerned regions, boroughs and rural districts, respectively, and did not, therefore, imply any principal change.

Voting right for regional council and municipal council is given to everyone in the region or primary municipality who has Danish citizenship, is 18 years old and has not been declared incapable. Scandinavian citizens who have lived 3 years in Denmark have also franchise.

Every voter is *eligible,* who has not been convicted of an act that in general opinion makes the person in question unworthy to be a member of the municipal council. One has simply to hand in a candidate list signed by at least 25 voters as supporters to be nominated as a candidate.

The municipal council elects its officers after the election every fourth year by electing a chairman, vice-chairman, committees, etc. Until 1970 the regional council's chairman was appointed by the monarch and the same was the case in the boroughs until 1919. The rural districts on the other hand had always elected their own chairman.

The number of council members in the primary municipalities on Funen varies between 11 and 29, while

119

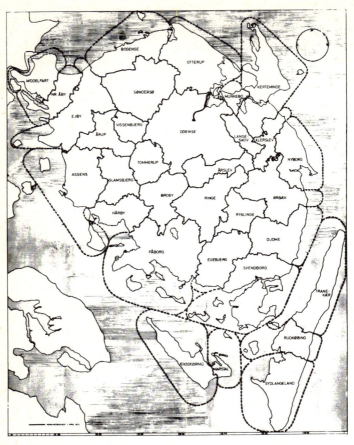

Outline map of the division of Funen into municipalities. 1/4/1970

the regional council has 27 members. The municipal council runs the municipal affairs according to administrative bye-laws that lay down the specific rules for each individual municipality.

All more important affairs, for example, the annual budget and all investments, are run by the council, but the

...rvesting. About half of the agricultural area of Funen is normally used to cultivate corn.

...th market gardening and fruit growing are important factors in the economic structure, and ...ong the fruit crops it is the apple that dominates all over the island.

Odense Steel Shipyard: The work of fitting out a large tanker is here seen through the window
the gantry crane driver's cab. The propeller for a 285,000 ton-tanker weighs about 57 tons

...rige-Titan A/S, Odense, is today an entirely Danish owned company employing about 1,200 ...ple in the field of industrial and marine services, D.C.-motors, motors for special purposes, ...escopic cranes, commutators, grinding machines, agricultural machinery, etc.

Aerial view of Roulunds Factories which also shows the test track which is an important par
the testing of the factory's car products, in particular brake linings.

Many busy ferry routes to and from Funen help to bind the Danish archipelago closer toget
Here a view of the big car ferry port Knudshoved south of Nyborg.

daily administration lies in the hands of the mayor and the committees with the help of the administrative personnel according to the administration's regulations. In Odense, where, as in the other big cities in the country there is a special "municipal organisation", the responsibility for the daily administration lies with the mayor and the 4 aldermen, each of whom has his municipal department.

The Constitution has not determined what the *responsibility* of the municipality is, and as a consequence this comes within the sphere of the municipality's independent organisation, but the responsibilities become evident by a series of statutory provisions and by long-term practice.

The responsibilities of the primary municipalities include the running of social welfare and health departments, schools and leisure activities, roads and sewage, as well as the provision of water, electricity and heating. The regional authorities cover the superior, communal responsibilities that concern hospitals, roads and water supplies, higher education, etc., as well as certain coordinating functions concerning, e.g., planning.

As a result of these duties both primary municipalities and regional authorities have the right to raise personal income tax and property tax. A large part of municipal expenses is covered, however, by grants from the Treasury according to various rules.

State supervision which governs the municipalities according to the Constitution means in effect for the primary municipalities in the first place a *board of control* with a chief administrative officer as chairman for every region. The *Home Office* functions as an appeal authority and supervises directly the regional councils. The Home Office and Board of Control deal only with legal matters and not with problems of expediency. Beyond this the government supervisory authorities are in the hands of the respective *ministers* with regard to, for example, school authorities, roads and environment.

In this connection one might also mention the *par-*

liamentary ombudsman, whose sphere of authority in the first place covers government services, but who can deal, to a certain extent, with complaints concerning municipal matters. His limitations with regards to the municipalities are connected with the fact that he can only deal with matters in which there is warrant for recourse to a government body and beyond that all the duties of the municipal authorities are not subject to the ombudsman. The ombudsman can, however, always investigate a case on his own initiative if there is any suspicion of violation of important legal interests.

Funen in Figures

by Bent Rygner

Funen is Denmark's second largest island; it is 3,000 km²
large, but one normally also includes the islands surrounding Funen. – In this way Funen and the surrounding islands
cover an area of about 3,500 km², that is about 8% of all of
Denmark which is c. 43,000 km² large. Langeland is the
largest of these islands at 300 km² in size and Tåsinge is the
second largest at about 70 km². There is a total of 25 inhabited and 72 uninhabited islands, which administratively
belong to the region of Funen.

By way of comparison it may be mentioned that the area
of Funen is almost double the size of London.

The region of Funen comprises 32 municipalities. In appendix 1 the names of the municipalities, area, population
on 1/1/1978 and the average area per inhabitant are mentioned. It appears from this that on average one person per
7,700 m² lives on Funen and in Denmark c. 8,400 m².
Funen is therefore slightly more densely populated than the
rest of the country, but there is a very great difference in
the population density of the individual municipalities. In
Odense there is only 1,800 m² and in Tranekær municipality (Langeland) c. 26,000 m² per head. By way of comparison it may be said that there is one person to 200 m² in
London.

The municipality of Odense has c. 168,000 inhabitants
and is thus the country's third largest city after Copenhagen
which has c. 516,000 and Århus with c. 243,000. In addition to the larger towns on Funen there are innumerable
built-up areas with about 1,000 or less inhabitants, while
along the country roads there are also many single farms
and houses, so that one gets the impression that the countryside is "inhabited". In 1976 the number of dwellings on

Appendix 1

The number of metres² per inhabitant per municipality

Town/ municipality	Area in km²	Population 1/1/78 rounded off	Average metres² per inhabitant rounded off
			1,000 m²
Assens	139	11,000	12.6
Bogense	102	6,200	16.4
Broby	100	6,500	16.2
Egebjerg	124	8,700	14.2
Ejby	163	10,100	16.1
Fåborg	227	17,800	12.8
Glamsbjerg	92	5,800	15.9
Gudme	120	6,500	18.6
Hårby	80	5,000	16.0
Kerteminde	143	10,400	13.8
Langeskov	43	5,800	7.5
Marstal	17	4,000	4.2
Middelfart	72	17,700	4.1
Munkebo	19	6,200	3.1
Nyborg	84	18,400	4.5
Nørre Åby	65	5,300	12.2
Odense	304	167,800	1.8
Otterup	169	11,200	15.0
Ringe	154	11,200	13.7
Rudkøbing	63	7,000	9.0
Ryslinge	82	6,700	12.1
Svendborg	173	37,300	4.6
Sydlangeland	121	5,300	22.9
Søndersø	181	11,200	16.3
Tommerup	73	6,900	10.6
Tranekær	107	4,100	26.0
Ullerslev	54	4,900	11.1
Vissenbjerg	47	5,900	8.0
Ærøskøbing	74	4,900	15.0
Ørbæk	138	6,600	21.0
Årslev	74	8,500	8.8
Årup	81	5,100	15.6
Total	3,485	450,000	7.7

Funen was calculated at c. 175,000, which means that on average 2.5 persons live per dwelling.

On Funen there are many manors, that is farms with an area of 200 hectares (2 km²) or more. There are 81 such manors on Funen, compared with 160 on Zealand, 57 on Lolland/Falster and 128 in Jutland; that is 426 altogether in Denmark. The largest manor on Funen is Wedellsborg, which is 4,000 hectares large and which is situated south of Middelfart, and the second largest is Tranekær Castle on Langeland at 3,300 hectares. In Jutland and on Zealand there are 4 manors in all that are larger than Wedellsborg in size.

The highest point on Funen, Frøbjerg Baunehøj, that lies south-west of Odense, is 131 m above sea-level. The highest points in Denmark, incidentally, are Yding Skovhøj, 173 m, and Ejer Baunehøj at 171 m, both lying south-west of Skanderborg in Jutland.

Two bridges have been built over the Lillebælt between Funen and Jutland, a combined railway and road bridge that is 825 m long and a six-lane road bridge, opened in 1970, which is 1,040 m long over the water and has an average height of 42 m. There is also an elevated bridge from Funen to Tåsinge and one from Tåsinge to Langeland. The plans to build a bridge from Funen over the island Sprogø in the Storebælt to Zealand have been suspended for economic reasons.

The distribution of the population in various age-groups is shown in appendix 2. The population of Funen including the surrounding islands makes up 8.8% of the Danish population. The distribution of the number of men and the number of women is the same as in the rest of the Danish population. On the other hand there are c. 6,000 fewer people in the 0–44 age-group, and c. 6,000 more in the 45 and above age-group on Funen, in comparison with the whole country.

Appendix 3 shows the population on Funen distributed according to employment, compared with the whole of

The population on Funen (1/1/1978) distributed according to age-group.

Age-groups	Funen Number	%	Entire country %	Funen x entire country's %
0–14 yrs	98,700	21.9	22.0	99,000
15–29 –	97,100	21.6	22.1	99,400
30–44 –	87,700	19.5	20.2	90,900
45–59 –	75,000	16.7	16.6	74,700
60–74 –	65,400	14.5	13.8	62,100
75–89 –	24,900	5.5	5.1	23,000
90 + –	1,200	0.3	0.2	900
Total	450,000	100.0	100.0	450,000

Denmark. The figures for agriculture and manufacturing are somewhat higher on Funen than in the entire country. One of the reasons is that apart from Copenhagen, Odense has the largest number of people employed in industry. As far as administration, diverse services and trades are concerned the Funen figures are, however, below average.

The Funen tax-payers' taxable income made up c. 6.5% of the entire country's income in 1977. At that time the average taxable income for the whole country was c. 44,300 kroner, while the inhabitant of Funen's was c. 40,000 kroner; yet the tax-payers of Munkebo municipality had the highest average taxable income on Funen, namely c. 43,300 kroner.

The population on Funen (1/7/1976) distributed according to economic groups and persons unemployed

	Funen Number	%	Entire country %	Funen x entire country's %
Agriculture, etc.	22,400	5.0	4.1	18,300
Manufacturing	49,700	11.1	9.6	42,900
Building and con-struction works	17,300	3.9	3.8	17,000
Trade and business	28,300	6.4	7.1	31,700
Transport and haulage ..	12,200	2.7	3.3	14,800
Administration and diverse services, trades ..	72,600	16.2	18.8	84,100
Unidentified	6,400	1.4	1.5	6,700
Total	208,900	46.7	48.2	215,500
Pensioners	73,000	16.3	15.2	68,000
Housewives	34,100	7.7	7.0	31,300
Children	106,500	23.8	23.9	106,800
Students, etc.	24,600	5.5	5.7	25,500
Total	238,200	53.3	51.8	231,600
Total	447,100	100.0	100.0	447,100

Economic Life

by Helge Sindal

In the latest survey of the total work force in Denmark it was reckoned that Funen and the islands around it had at its disposal over 214,897 employed people. This is 8.6% of the total work force in the country.

It is possible to gain a rough impression of the position of Funen in the total national economic structure through the figures on page 129, which partly show the break-up of the major economic groups on Funen and in the whole of Denmark and partly show other parts of the country that are placed highest and lowest, respectively, in each group.

If one is especially interested in the four largest economic groups, these figures spell out that the centre of gravity in the economic life on Funen today is to be found in manufacturing, that is, industry and trade.

As far as agriculture, market gardening, fishery etc. are concerned "the green island" is still above average, but included in these figures is also the wide-ranging area covered by the capital city. Compared with the more scanty land in Jutland, the fertile soil of Funen provides work for far fewer than one would imagine.

Agriculture

About half of the agricultural area of Funen is normally used to cultivate corn and by far the largest part of that land is used for feeding purposes; consequently, it is barley and oats that dominate.

A special crop on Funen is buckwheat, the grain of which is used for the production of the traditional and highly praised buckwheat porridge. Even though this crop only

The distribution of the work force in %, October 1975

		Funen	Denmark
Agriculture, market gardening, fishery, etc.		11.9	9.2
highest: Viborg region	21.2		
lowest: Copenhagen–Frederiksberg	0.2		
Manufacturing		29.2	25.5
highest: Vejle region	31.1		
lowest: Bornholm	18.7		
Building and construction works		8.2	8.1
highest: West Zealand	10.6		
lowest: Copenhagen–Frederiksberg	4.9		
Trade and business		14.4	15.5
highest: Copenhagen region	19.4		
lowest: Viborg region	12.0		
Transport and haulage		5.4	6.5
highest: Copenhagen–Frederiksberg	9.0		
lowest: Viborg region	4.1		
Administration, teaching, social/health departments		23.8	27.8
highest: Frederiksborg region	35.5		
lowest: Ringkøbing region	21.3		
Diverse services, trades		5.5	5.6
highest: Copenhagen–Frederiksberg	7.2		
lowest: Southern Jutland	4.8		
Unidentified, conscripts		1.6	1.8
highest: Copenhagen–Frederiksberg	2.4		
lowest: Bornholm	1.3		

plays a relatively modest part, compared with the wide-spread cultivation in other parts of the world, e.g., Russia, every Dane will without hesitation associate it with Funen. There has been created a very humorous association of fanatical Funen-dwellers, SEBOFIFS, the Society for the Promotion of Buckwheat Eating in the Diocese of Funen, which along with the display of hilarious rituals and the due favour of the press, pays homage to this tradition of Funen.

Amongst the root crops it is fodder beets and sugarbeets that are the most popular. The sugar refinery is at Assens.

Cattle breeding on Funen is dominated by the Red Danes (Danish milch cow), which was introduced into Funen in the period after 1840 and today it is the most wide-spread breed found in Denmark. This again implies that milk products, like butter and cheese, are of considerable importance. In addition, within the sphere of cheese production there is a particular speciality from Funen, namely smoked cheese, which just has to be from Funen if it is to be perfect.

Pig-breeding plays an important part as well. A large part of the pigs end up, via the large abattoirs of Funen, on Danish or foreign dinner tables, but Funen has made a name for itself in the area of breed improvement and therefore exports many live pigs as well. In addition Funen is the home of widespread poultry breeding which does not only include hens but also ducks and geese.

Market Gardening and Fruit Growing

The good soil of Funen and the mild, friendly climate naturally lead to the fact that both market gardening and the growing of fruit is an important factor in the economic structure, partly in the form of independent enterprises and partly as a sideline to agriculture.

There are market gardens all over Funen, but the central area for this branch of the occupation is certainly the area around Odense. Here one can find – especially north of the

130

city – widespread areas with vegetables in the open and in the many greenhouses.

Among the fruitcrops it is the apple that dominates all over the island. It is an impressive sight in the latter part of May, not least in South Funen, to see the many hundred thousands of fruit trees in blossom.

Finally, there are many places on Funen that are set apart for seed growing and this, together with the many other blossoming crops, makes just the right conditions for a significant bee-keeping, even though the intensive use in recent times of spraying poison has given bee-keeping a set-back.

Fishery

The greatest part of the fishery yields from Funen goes to the island's own use and it is only a relatively small amount that is now and then sold beyond the island. The most important fishing harbours are Kerteminde, Svendborg, Nyborg, Rudkøbing, Lohals and Bagenkop.

Forestry

Forestry does not play any significant role in the economy of Funen. The most important plantations lie in South Funen and belong to the large estates.

Industry and Trade

Certain branches of industry have already been named in connection with the reference to agriculture, such as abattoirs and sugar factories. There are, however, many more industrial concerns that refine agricultural products, such as breweries, of which by far the largest is Albani in Odense, mills and conserving and canning factories.

Yet in spite of this the entire food and drink industry on Funen accounts for only about 1/6 of the total personnel employed in industry in the region of Funen. The "heaviest" and most important branch of industry is without doubt the iron and metal industry that employs 20,000 or 1/2 of the total 40,000 that work in manufacturing industries of one or the other type. Just under 1/3 of these are women. There are c. 7,500 works in all with a total turn-over of c. 14 billion Danish kroner. The largest works in iron and steel is the Lindø shipyard north of Odense and Thrige-Titan and Haustrup in Odense.

There are altogether 10 works that employ over 500; this means that the manufacturing works on Funen are characterized by what has been called an "undergrowth" of small and medium-sized concerns that to a large extent function as sub-contractors to the few large works. There are, therefore, many smaller places of employment, but they are often extremely dependent on market trends and marketing possibilities of the few giants.

One of the important problems for those who work to create a more stable state of the market in industry in the region of Funen – not least after the impact of the world-wide energy crisis since 1973 – is precisely, therefore, to ensure a more constant and less vulnerable market. This may presumably ensure in particular that more small and medium-sized industries are in a position to establish independent export to a large number of foreign markets.

Shipping

The region of Funen, being surrounded by water, has naturally been important from ancient times for sea transport. This covers both shipbuilding, with many large and small yards producing fine quality new ships to both Danish and foreign shipping companies, and also the shipping business, which today, however, is dominated by the state-run ferry transport. Many busy ferry routes to and from Funen help to bind the Danish archipelago closer together. There are now altogether two bridges between

Funen and Jutland and there is also a bridge to Tåsinge and to Langeland, but the long-planned bridge connection to Zealand and Copenhagen over the Storebælt is now shelved, because of economic problems; that means, of course, that the ferry traffic will continue to play an all-important role, not only for Funen, but for all of Denmark.

For the commercial life of Funen the lack of a complete system of bridge connections in Denmark means increased costs in the marketing of finished products around the country. It involves increased competition which in the long and short terms can prove to be extremely serious.

Business and Trade

Odense in particular but also other towns on Funen have for innumerable generations functioned as influential centres of business not only in the internal trade of the island, but also throughout the country and at an international level.

There are c. 6,500 businesses on Funen and they have a total annual turn-over of c. 10 billion kroner. Trade, therefore, is the most important branch of industry after manufacturing works in industry and handicrafts, as far as financial turn-over is concerned.

Two great figures in Danish business life, C. F. Tietgen (1829–1901) and Thomas B. Thrige (1866–1938), were both from Funen and both born in Odense. While Tietgen, as a financier and a man of vision, worked on a world-wide scale at a national and international level, Thomas B. Thrige's work was closely connected with his childhood town, Odense, where he built up a large industrial concern, to which his name is connected, and which he handed over to one of Denmark's most distinguished foundations which also bears his name.

The Muses Flourish

by Aksel Brahe

It is a claim not utterly unfounded that the people on Hans Christian Andersen's and Carl Nielsen's island of birth, as is often maintained, should be more disposed towards art and music than in other parts of the country – though comparisons in this field can be difficult. In any case it is a fact that the breadth of cultural offers on Funen, centred around Odense, is exceptionally great, and that these opportunities are increasingly exploited by all age groups, especially perhaps by the young public.

In the area of drama the natural centre is Odense Theatre, which consists of a large and a smaller theatre, the latter suited for more experimental drama. At the moment the theatre is visited by over 100,000 from Funen per season with the numbers ever increasing. In addition to this concrete proof of interest in the theatre in the provinces, the actors can enjoy new and improved settings in which to perform. A few years ago the theatre building in Jernbanegade, which was first used in 1913, received major reconstruction which provided more room in many areas and therefore increased the possible repertoire. Among other things the orchestra pit was extended so that it is now possible, unlike previously, to perform major operas with full orchestration.

At the same time Odense Theatre was reconstructed it received a new leader, the young Waage Sandø, who succeeded the regional theatre leader of the previous 17 years, Kai Wilton. There was a change of a whole generation, as far as the age of the leader was concerned and, at the same time to a certain extent, a similar change in the repertoire, as the new leader has a reputation for choosing more modern, socially-engaged drama, yet still within the scope of the commitments a provincial theatre is subject to, namely to perform a well-balanced, cultural and entertaining repertoire.

Attached to the 180 year old theatre is a School of Dramatic Art which is considered one of the country's best; this is demonstrated by the fact that ten times as many pupils as can possibly be accepted apply for entry. The school, which is led by the actress Grethe Holmer, has a well developed teaching staff both Danish and foreign; one of the foreign teachers, for example, is the internationally famous East German actress Gisela May. Many of the pupils graduating from the school receive their "baptism of fire" in musical productions that Odense Theatre has a particular knack of doing well.

In recent years the theatre has made a great effort to reach the public by performing all over Funen in more or less untraditional premises, often followed by a debate with the audience about what they have watched. A special effort is made to interest the very young in the theatrical arts by Funen's School Theatre which presents its own performances every season, often dramatisations of known children's and young people's books.

At the same time there are theatrical performances on many other levels than professional. For example, there has been for 30 years an amateur theatre in Odense, ODF Theatre, which from a modest beginning has grown to an institution that is highly esteemed. All through the season public performances are given in addition to a large study group project, and, as an example of the artistic standard one might mention the fact that the theatre every now and then releases a member to one of the professional theatres.

A new initiative in the theatre life of Funen is the establishment of the theatre "Ask og Embla" (the name comes from Norse mythology) in Odense's new pedestrian precinct, Vintapperstræde. It is a theatre, started by a group of young theatre people and teachers, that stresses experimental genres and thereby carries out drama research. In addition attention is paid to children and young people with a series of performances.

There are plans meanwhile for the establishment of a second children's and young people's theatre with regional support in Odense, an initiative that has evolved from a children's theatre festival in the city in 1978. It must be said that they are a section of the public that is in the good graces of the theatre personnel.

In Svendborg there is the "Baggårdsteater", a young group that originally began on an amateur basis, but now has the status of regional theatre and performs all over Funen; on a less serious level the people of Funen and tourists are entertained in the summer by "Rottefælden" (the Rat trap) which is 95 years old and the country's oldest permanent revue theatre, also its richest in tradition.

Two open air summer performances should be included in the theatre life of Funen, that each year attract large audiences. One is the Hans Christian Andersen Play in the "Funen Village" (Open air museum) in Odense, in which professional and amateur actors present dramatisations of the fairy-tale author's most famous tales, and the second is the "Voldspil" (Ramparts Play) in Nyborg which has a popular musical or operetta on its programme every year, performed in the idyllic surroundings by the ancient Nyborg Castle.

Masses of Music

Odense City Orchestra is undoubtedly the mainstay in the field of music in the region of Funen and is an institution that is also gradually on its way to make an international reputation for itself.

It began in 1976 when they were on tour in West Germany, Holland and Belgium and were exceptionally successful everywhere they went by playing *inter alia* the music of the Danish national composer, Carl Nielsen. It is the first

136

To all appearances the village consists of wandering from bed to table, from work to inn, from street corner to gossiping over coffee. But indoors they read books, recite poetry and go in for singing, music and sport.

provincial orchestra here to have travelled abroad and in 1981 the Funen orchestra is invited on a new tourné, this time to the Soviet Union.

The city orchestra's artistic leader for the past ten years has been the Polish conductor Karol Stryja who is the leader of Katowice's Symphony Orchestra, which is considered Poland's best, in addition to his job in Odense. It is therefore a first-rate man whom they have managed to get as the leader of the provincial orchestra of Funen, and this is confirmed by the fact that his name and international connections have made it possible in recent seasons to attract a large number of important soloists and conductors to Odense – artists who would not have included Denmark in their travels, if they had not known Stryja.

The second conductor in the city orchestra is Børge Wagner, originally a hornist, who became a conductor a number of years ago and who has also contributed to the high artistic standard which the orchestra has built up gradually.

As an example of the surplus capacity that exists in the orchestra one might mention the fact that three chamber music ensembles have grown out of it, Pro Musica, the Carl

Nielsen quartet, named after the famous composer who had his roots in Funen, and the Funen Trio – all giving frequent concerts on Funen, in addition to the fact that many orchestra members are also teachers in the Music Conservatory of Funen.

There has started a new tradition in the city in the summer season, a "Multi-Music-Festival" in which both instrumental and vocal music of all types is performed – jazz-beat, folk music, brass bands and light music. It takes place in all sorts of different premises all over Odense, indoors and outdoors – all free of charge as an extra summer benefit from municipality and region. In 1978 there were as many as 82 events in a period of nine days.

If you want to relax to more restful music as a concert attender or tourist, then there is a series of concerts arranged every summer in the churches of Odense, as many as c. 30, while those specially interested in jazz can cultivate their hobby in the city's jazz house "Sophus Ferdinand".

In the field of amateur music the region of Funen can offer Funen's Amateur Symphony Orchestra and a large number of choirs, of which undoubtly the most proficient is St. Knud's Gymnasium Choir in Odense, which is conducted by Carsten Mollerup and which, for example, has won a number of song contests on Denmark's Radio. Carsten Mollerup, aided by his wife, Inga Mollerup, also took the initiative to create a new form of concert in the Town Hall of Odense, "Sing Along Together", in which the choir has been extremely successful at singing together with the audience songs appropriate to the season four times a year, always with a large attendance.

Outside of Odense one must mention the summer concerts at Egeskov Castle in mid-Funen to which Count Gregers Ahlefeldt-Laurvig invites every year first-class soloists and ensembles to concerts in the great hall, which with its august age – c. 500 years old – and historical decor must be said to be without comparison the most distinguished concert hall on Funen. In any case the castle is one of Funen's

...ense Theatre, the regional theatre of Funen which has recently been rebuilt and expanded.

...ft: The theatre workshop in the Odense Theatre devotes itself largely to experimental drama. ...re is a scene from "Piger i hvidt" (Girls in white), a play that looks closely at the situation of ...men today.

...ght: A scene from Odense Theatre's production of the play "Ventetid" (Waiting time) by the ...erican playwright Michael Christofer; it is about people's reactions to death by cancer.

Left: Odense Theatre's director, Waage Sandø.
Right: Karol Stryja, Odense City Symphony Orchestra's Polish-born senior conductor.

The Odense City Symphony Orchestra.

ır world-famous natives of Funen, clockwise:
e physicist Hans Christian Ørsted (1777–1851), the philologist Rasmus Kristian Rask
87–1832), the writer Hans Christian Andersen (1805–75) and the composer Carl Nielsen
65–1931).

The Hans Christian Andersen district in Odense, reconstructed in 1970–75 by the architects E. & E. Lehn Petersen.

The Hans Christian Andersen Museum, Odense, built 1974–76. Design architect Ebbe Lehn Petersen. Entrance.

three-star tourist attractions and these concerts have made it even more attractive.

A project that will be of exceptional importance for the music life of Funen is at present in preparation and will be completed in 1980; it is a new, modern concert hall that is being erected on *Sortebrødre* Square in Odense's centre at a price of around 50 million kroner (over £5 million) and with room for 1200 of an audience. The concert hall will primarily be the home of the Odense City Orchestra, which has had to play for many years in premises which are not really intended for concerts – Funen's Community Centre and the Odense Town Hall. This has not affected the artistic standard, but there has been inferior acoustics and service for the public in these premises, and this is what is now being paid attention to. It is a project that will offer great possibilities to the musical life on Funen, not only as a centre for the more established musical activities, but also to a large extent for the development of the lighter types of music – jazz, beat, etc., which up till now, when there's been a large arrangement, have been directed to Funen's Forum, Odense's large community centre, which was pulled down a short time ago because it was so antiquated.

In the same year as the new concert hall will be completed – 1980 – Odense will be the setting for yet another large musical event: The First International Carl Nielsen Competition for young violinists. Queen Margrethe has expressed her willingness to be the patron of this musical trial of strength, that will be followed up in the following years, and well-known adjudicators can be expected to ensure that the competition will keep the high standard that is being aimed at. The president of the board of adjudicators will be the Polish-born violin virtuoso, Henryk Szeryng, now living in Mexico, and as vice-president has been chosen the equally well-known Czech violinist, Josef Suk, grandson of the composer of the same name and great-grandson of Antonin Dvorak. Three more members will be brought in from abroad, the American violin teacher,

Joseph Glingold, the internationally famous Soviet violinist, Leonid Kogan, and his Norwegian colleague, Arve Tellefsen. If the competition is a success, it is hoped that a tradition will be created that will establish the name of Odense on an international level as a city of music, and at the same time build up increased attention to the leading Danish composer, as the different competition pieces will be compositions by Carl Nielsen with his violin concerto as the great, final contest.

Travelling on Funen

by Knud Secher

Where did the island of Funen get its name from? Researchers in folklore and history have presented many different answers to that question. When the island's world-renowned son, the author Hans Christian Andersen expressed *his* opinion, he did it naturally in a poetic vein:

> "Navnet *Fyn* betyder *fin* og vil så meget sige,
> at Fyn, det er en have fin for hele Danmarks rige"
> (The name of Funen means "fine" and means in so many words,
> That Funen is a fine garden for the entire kingdom of Denmark).

Denmark's garden – this expression has also been used by many other Danish poets who, naturally, like Andersen, have combined by these words something beautiful, idealistic, well-kept – a quite special tone, inspired by the nature of Funen, landscape and the national mentality; this can be recognized time after time both in Andersen's writing and in the other world famous native of Funen, Carl Nielsen's music.

Funen has naturally also an advantage as a holiday resort with its position in the centre of Denmark, in, as they say, the "hub" of the country. It is easy and convenient to reach Funen from all parts of Denmark, by rail, plane and ship. The main railway from Nyborg through Odense to Middelfart connects Copenhagen and Zealand with Jutland and consequently with the rest of Scandinavia and countries south of Denmark. Funen and Jutland are connected by two bridges, a railway bridge and a motorway bridge, and there are plans, which probably will not be realized in the near future, to build "the world's longest bridge", which would connect Zealand and Funen and supplant the existing ferry connections. This gigantic project that will naturally try the engineers' abilities to the utmost and be a great burden on the country's economy, provides in these years the arena for a spirited political debate. Bridges and ferries connect Funen also with the islands to the south.

The continually increasing number of tourists that come by yacht can find berths in the marinas that are appearing with the same rapid speed; these marinas are to be found both in the coastal towns on Funen and in the so-called South Funen archipelago.

In the middle of the "hub" lies the capital of Funen, Odense, and one cannot mention the town without mentioning Hans Christian Andersen. Odense is indeed a lively, enterprising industrial city with about 170,000 inhabitants, but so many tourists choose Odense first and foremost as tourist resort, because it is the famous author's home town and the home of the unique collections in the Hans Christian Andersen Museum. Every year between 150,000 and 200,000 tourists visit this museum and many the little, half-timbered house in Munkemøllestræde where the poet spent some of his childhood years.

The *Hans Christian Andersen Museum* was built in 1905 when the centenary of the writer's birth was celebrated all over Denmark. The city of Odense decided on that occasion to donate a museum to the memory of its famous son, who was also an honorary freeman of the city, and they obtained for the purpose the little house on the corner of Hans Jensensstræde and Bangs Boder. Hans Christian Andersen did not himself know precisely in which of the houses in the neighbourhood he saw the light of day for the first time. When he was born on April 2, 1805, his very poor parents had no permanent home. It was not until many years later, around the time when Andersen was elected freeman of the city, that this house was singled out as his place of birth, with the backing of oral tradition. Since then it has been shown that in the years around 1805

Andersen's grandmother, then later a female relation, rented the house.

In 1905 the city of Odense had this building renovated and in so doing tried to restore its original exterior, while making the interior suitable for its use as a museum. The increase in the collections and an enormous increase in visitors has made it necessary to enlarge it twice. In 1930, 125 years after the writer's birth, additions were made to the west and south of the original museum building and in the corner a large domed hall was built, in which the marvellous frescoes of Niels Larsen Stevns reproduce important periods in Hans Christian Andersen's life. In 1975, the centenary of Andersen's death, the area of the museum was doubled by the addition of new buildings in continuation of the domed hall with a facade that faces on to an earlier, very beautiful and idyllic park area. After these extensions Hans Christian Andersen's house now appears as a museum of world importance.

At the same time the municipality has seen to it in most recent years that the small, single-storey houses around the museum have been restored, houses that would otherwise have disappeared, and given them new interiors, so that the whole neighbourhood appears now just as it did in the writer's childhood and will remain so in future centuries.

If the visitor takes sufficient time – and that would be two or three hours – to examine the museum and perhaps supplement this afterwards with a short visit to his childhood home in Munkemøllestræde, he will continue his journey with an unforgettable impression of Andersen as a man, the dissemination of his writings over the entire world and the fairy tale world into which he led his readers, both children and adults. Furthermore, if one is particularly interested one can find in a little street not far from the museum, called Påskestræde, the spot near Odense River where the writer's mother washed clothes. Hans Christian Andersen's childhood and early youth were spent in straitened circumstances, which is clearly reflected in his

143

work. He experienced, as he himself said, such awful times and became famous.

There are many other museums in Odense – a newly established railway museum, amongst others, and, as the greatest attraction in addition to the Hans Christian Andersen Museum, the Funen Village (the open air museum of rural buildings) in the outskirts of the town. In this museum, built in the years when the Second World War raged, a series of typical farms and buildings from different villages on Funen has been collected and in this way a unique reminder of peasant culture on Funen has been created. Every year well over 100,000 visitors come to this museum.

In present-day Odense the administration, organisation, tourist boards, etc. place great importance on presenting an image other than that of museums. The town's large industrial plants are stressed and attention is called to one of the world's largest shipyards, Lindø Shipyard, in which have been built some of our era's largest supertankers that sail the seven seas. It is such a concern that makes one think of the following lines of Hans Christian Andersen's beautiful national song: "I am born in Denmark and there I have my home"

> Once you were lords of all the North,
> Ruled over England, now you are called weak,
> A little land, and yet the Dane's song and chisel stroke
> Are heard so far round the world.

One is naturally aware in Odense that it is Hans Christian Andersen's name that is the magnet that attracts the great stream of tourists to Funen and therefore to the entire island. In the height of the summer a Hans Christian Andersen play is performed in the Funen Village's attractive theatre, a play built on one of Hans Christian Andersen's fairy tales and almost entirely performed by children. Near the Hans Christian Andersen Museum is at present being constructed a large new concert and congress building. It is named after the town's and the region's second, world-famous son, the composer Carl Nielsen.

Carl Nielsen was born in a little village near Odense, Nørre Lyndelse, where his father who was a master painter and village musician, gave him his first violin lessons and took him along when there was dance music in the village hall. When Carl Nielsen was only 14 he became an army musician in Odense and four years later he began his education at the Royal Danish Music Conservatory in Copenhagen, where several of the first-class talents of the Danish world of music had at that stage spotted his unique talent. Later he was a violinist in the Royal Theatre orchestra while beginning to compose at the same time. Many years passed, however, before Carl Nielsen won the international reputation he now enjoys. As a composer he was really before his time, an expression he himself would not have accepted, as he always considered music to be timeless. Now his symphonies and works are played all over the world, e.g., Leonard Bernstein has presented them in many concert halls in U.S.A. and other countries.

As a composer Carl Nielsen is typically Danish; he was not influenced by the great, foreign composers, but rather by earlier Danish ones, who, however, had never reached his status or artistic greatness. He never forgot either that he had his roots in Funen and one of his most frequently performed works is the Song Cycle "Fynsk Forår" (Springtime on Funen), which is directly inspired by the impressions he received from his childhood and youth in the Funen environment. Carl Nielsen has also put music to a number of the most sung and beloved Danish songs.

A little house in Nørre Lyndelse where Carl Nielsen lived from the age of 7 to 14 has now been converted into a museum and the little village cherishes his memory with great reverence.

In another little village near Odense, Brændekilde, the philologist Rasmus Kristian Rask was born, who today, over 150 years after his death, is considered one of the founders of modern comparative philology. His dissertations on many different languages were pioneer studies in philology. Rask was strongly nationalistic all of his life and wrote practically all his works in Danish. In 1825 he refused an offer of a position abroad and made on that occasion the statement that has since been frequently repeated: "One owes everything one can achieve to one's native land".

The coastal towns of Funen have become a favourite port of call not least after the fantastic increase in the number of tourists who come by yacht. All these towns have historical local colour and modern facilities to offer, while most of them have established museums and collections, where relics of the past are preserved.

Assens is a very old town and although its age is unknown, we do know that it was named for the first time in King Valdemar II's Doomsday Book of 1231. The town's oldest building, Vor Frue Church, was completed in c. 1488. One of the most beautiful houses in the town is the birthplace of the naval hero, Peder Willemoes, and it is over 300 years old, but there are many beautiful, old houses and large merchants' houses in addition in Assens, as in all the market towns of Funen.

Bogense is Funen's smallest market town and one of the country's most idyllic coastal towns. It received its town privileges in 1288. A certain degree of stagnation in the business life of the town is countered by an exceptionally well developed tourist life, concentrated on the large, newly built marina.

The town of *Middelfart,* lying near the Lillebælt and the two bridges that lead to Jutland, grew into being about 1000 years ago with the name Mæthelfart around an old royal castle, "Gorm's Castle".

To the east, as a harbour for the Storebælt, lies *Nyborg* with its greatest attraction Nyborg Castle, built in 1170, Scandinavia's oldest royal palace. In the Middle Ages

Nyborg was the capital of the country, because of its central position in the middle of the kingdom and its natural harbour in the fjord.

Ringe, in the middle of Funen, is, because of its position, among other things, the natural point of departure for excursions into the centre of Hans Christian Andersen's "Garden of Funen". In all directions you come to the region's tourists' jewels, the picturesque wind and water mills and the manor houses of Egeskov, Sandholt, Brobygaard, Ravnholt and Lykkesholm, as well as Hvidkilde near Svendborg and Valdemar's Castle on the little island Tåsinge, south of Svendborg, which are among the best preserved in Denmark. Many of these castles and manor houses have been opened to the public, in British fashion, and in many the owners have set up cafeterias and special exhibitions.

Svendborg is Funen's second largest town with 37,000 inhabitants and the capital of South Funen. Svendborg was first mentioned in 1229 but had been an important settlement and centre for shipping long before that. The town has still a strong connection with the Danish merchant fleet and is the home of navigation schools and ship and boat yards of all kinds. The poet Johannes Jørgensen, whose work is especially known in the Catholic world, was born in Svendborg and was made an honorary freeman of the town.

The islands to the south of Funen are also the centre in the high season for thousands upon thousands of tourists who either sail there in their own boats along the many shipping channels from Germany and between the islands of Funen, or come over the bridges that today link some of the islands with the "mainland" of Funen.

Via one of these bridges one can drive from Svendborg, over the little island of *Tåsinge,* the scene of the Danish Mayerling drama with the joint suicide of the circus girl Elvira Madigan and the Swedish Count Sparre, on to the larger, very elongated island that fittingly bears the name of

Langeland (Longland). Adam Oehlenschläger, the poet and composer of the Danish national anthem, called Langeland "a rose sprig in the sea".

In the capital of Langeland, *Rudkøbing,* two famous Danes were born about two hundred years ago – the Ørsted brothers, Anders Sandø Ørsted, Denmark's most prominant lawyer and Hans Christian Ørsted, who in 1820 proved that an electric current can turn a magnetic needle, a discovery that created the basis for modern electromagneticism and made Ørsted's name world famous. In 1850 his most important philosophical work, "Aanden i Naturen" (the Spirit in Nature), that had a great impact on his age, was published in many editions and translated into many languages.

Even though modern tourism, at least in the summer, has made an entry, for good or bad, onto the island of *Ærø,* the archipelago's doorway to the south, one finds a particularly characteristic piece of the early history of Denmark – idyllic villages with old half-timbered farms alternate with interesting churches, archaeological relics of early history and unusually well-preserved relics of a market town, and everything, as Ærø is certainly not large, has the bracing Baltic as a background.

The island's two towns, *Marstal* and *Ærøskøbing*, vie with each other, often not at all in a peaceful and harmonious way, for the honour of being the island's "capital". *Marstal,* a town of 4,000 inhabitants, is very strongly influenced by its affiliations with ocean seafaring and shipping, in early times with sailing ships and in the present day with modern merchant fleets. Marstal still has shipyards and a large new and attractive navigational school. Here and at the navigational school at Svendborg thousands of young people are educated who today and in the future will help maintain the Danish reputation of being a seafaring nation.

This reputation, yet in another context, reminds one to visit the *Ladby* find between Odense and Kerteminde. Not so many years ago a man's grave dating from the Viking era, c. 900 A.D. was discovered and excavated here. The dead man was buried in a mound in a ship that was c. 21 m. long, and 3 m. broad at the centre, along with horses, dogs and other possessions. The grave was plundered and only the iron parts and impressions of wood were found. These relics are preserved, while the major part of the rest of the find can be seen in Denmark's National Museum (in Copenhagen).

At that point in the Second World War when there was much talk about a German invasion of England, a group of German officers visited the Ladby ship. Their Danish guide, who must have had a good share of Funen humour, said with a roguish smile to one of the Germans: "It was with such ships we conquered England. But you see, we were able to do so!". Surprisingly the guide escaped unpunished from this unheard of insult to the German fighting forces!

But, back to Ærø, the island's second large town, *Ærøskøbing,* has only 1200 inhabitants, but is one of Denmark's best preserved market towns with 36 listed buildings. Ærøskøbing's beautiful old townhall is the only one in Denmark that has permission to fly the swallow-tailed flag with royal initials, as a token of thanks for the island's loyality to Denmark under foreign rule. This special permission is renewed with every change of Monarch in Denmark.

Ærøskøbing's population is decreasing, while on the other hand the town and its surrounding area is considered to be increasing steadily in the number of tourists especially from Germany. And in Ærøskøbing, the fairy tale town as it is called, they come to an idyllic place and surroundings that could not be more genuinely Danish.

The Authors

Gorm Benzon, born 1929. Trained with the Hørsholm Newspaper in 1952, then employed by the Frederiksborg Amtstidende and Ekstrabladet papers. Attached to Politiken newspaper from 1962–71 as their correspondent on antiques. Since then has worked exclusively as an author, and has published a large number of books on cultural history, e.g., "Antiques and Curiosities", "Gyldendal's Antique Handbook", Vol. 17 of "Danish Castles and Manors", "Our Ancient Churches and Monasteries", and has recently written a book on ancient Danish doors.

Aksel Brahe, born 1934, journalist with the Fyens Stiftstidende newspaper in Odense. Trained with Grenå Folketidende in 1954, after which he was employed by a number of newspapers in the provinces and Information in Copenhagen; from 1965 connected to Fyens Stiftstidende, specializing in cultural affairs.

Peter Eriksen, born 1930, journalist since 1947. Employed by Fyens Stiftstidende in Odense as editor of the back page. Has made guest appearances in talk programmes on Funen's regional radio, in societies as lecturer, and for many years has been co-author of a series of revues and cabarets in Danish theatre.

Viggo Land, born 1913. Teacher training certificate in 1935, school consultant for Odense and Assens' county councils in 1951, administrative chief of the educational and cultural departments of the Funen regional authorities from 1971–1978.

Ebbe Lehn Petersen, born 1928. Graduated from Odense Katedralskole in 1946, and the Art Academy's School of Architecture in 1953. Ran an architectural business in collaboration with his father Knud Lehn Petersen and brother Erik Lehn Petersen from 1955–1974. After their death has run the company alone.

150

Hugo Mayntzhusen, born 1918. Graduated from Aalborg Katedralskole in 1936, cand.jur. 1943, deputy judge in Thisted the same year, appointed to the Ministry of the Interior 1945, Assistant Secretary 1960, Director of Municipal Authorities the same year.

Henning Nielsen, born 1952. M.A. (history and Danish), Grammar School teacher. Has written, e.g. *Det Fynske Itri* A historical-topographical description of Vissenbjerg parish, 1971, co-author of "Houses worthy of Conservation in Svendborg", 1975. Contributor to the project Odense City's History. Odense University Gold Medal 1977 for a thesis "Danish Foreign Politics 1875–1894" (published 1977).

Anne Okkels Olsen, M.A. (history and philosophy), teacher at the Funen Region New Gymnasium (Grammar School). Has previously written contributions to the historical section of the North Funen and South Funen's volumes of "Gyldendal's Account of the Regions".

Bente Rosenbeck, M.A. (history and philosophy) from Odense University in 1976. Lecturer at the OUC (Odense University Centre), specializing in feminist studies.

Bent Rygner, graduated from Odense Katedralskole in 1935. Commercial science certificate (HA) 1938, commercial science diploma (HD) 1942, degree in commercial studies, Copenhagen Commercial College 1955. Since 1956 employed by Odense municipality as head of the Statistics Office.

Knud Secher, born 1907, journalist. Worked with a number of Danish newspapers. Editor of Fyens Stiftstidende, Funen's largest newspaper, from 1936–45; editor-in-chief from 1945–76. Author of several collections of poems, biographies, and novels.

Helge Sindal, born 1938. Degree in economics 1961. Lecturer at Aalborg Commercial School 1962–68. Inspector in the Ministry of Education 1968–71. Director of Tietgenskolen in Odense since 1971. Chairman of the Labour Market Board in the Region of Funen 1978.

Finn Stendal Pedersen, born 1943. M.A. (history and religious studies), appointed at Odense University as lecturer in 1970. Member of the Agricultural Historical Society and committee member of the Funen Region's Historical Society. Member of the Danish Students' Joint Council chairmanship 1965–67, chairman of the Students' Council of Århus University 1967–68. Has produced teaching material and source pamphlets concerning Danish agricultural history c. 1650–1800.

Carsten Tofte, born 1930. Graduated from the Danish School of Librarianship 1975. City librarian for Odense Central Library since 1976.

152

Illustrations

(a) above, (b) below

Gregers Ahlefeldt-Laurvig, Egeskov: Cover, flyleaf, plate 23
AiO Tryk as, Odense: plates 4, 5, 6, 7, 8 (Wermund Bendtsen)
Ole Akhøj: plate 3
Hans Christian Andersen Museum: plate 51(b)
Aschehoug Publishers, Copenhagen (from "Fynske Jernbaner"):
    plate 9(a)
Wermund Bendtsen: plate 28(b)
Stig Benzon: page 53, plates 10(a), 13(b), 17, 18(a), 19, 20(b),
    22(b), 24, 25(b), 26
Kai C, Fyens Stiftstidende: drawings page 9, 13, 83, 99, 137
CowiConsult, Virum: plate 2(a)
Døveskolernes Materialelaboratorium 42 (b)
Chr. Erichsen Publishers, Copenhagen (from "H. C. Andersens
    Eventyr" 1 + 2): page 31
Fyns Pressefoto: plates 10(b), 11, 12(b), 15(b), 44, 45, 48(b),
    37(a), 40
Sylvest Jensens Luftfoto: plate 38/39
Krohn & Hartvig Rasmussen 29 (b)
Lone Mengel: plates 30(b), 32, 52
Poul Olsen: plate 42(a)
Jørgen Outzen 43
Thomas Pedersen: plate 29(a)
The Royal Academy of Arts' Library, Copenhagen: plate 27(a)
    right
The Royal Library, Copenhagen: plate 51
Svendborg Tourist Association: plate 2(b)
Ellen Thoby: plates 12(a), 14, 15(a), 20(a), 21, 22(a), 25(a)
D. Williams: plate 1
Ib Withen: page 4, Map of the Island Region of Funen

and others

Index

The letters *æ, ø, å* (in that order) follow *z* in the Danish alphabet and entries containing these special Danish vowel signs are alphabetized accordingly; *aa* is identical with *å*. Numbers in italics indicate plate numbers.

157

DET DANSKE SELSKAB

The Danish Institute for Information about Denmark and Cultural Cooperation with other Nations

KULTORVET 2, DK-1175 COPENHAGEN, DENMARK

Publications in English:

DANISH INFORMATION HANDBOOKS

Schools and Education – The Danish Folk High Schools – Special Education in Denmark – Public Libraries in Denmark – Social Welfare in Denmark – Local Government in Denmark – The Danish Cooperative Movement

DENMARK IN PRINT AND PICTURES

The Danish Church – Danish Architecture – Danish Painting and Sculpture – Danish Design – Industrial Life in Denmark – The Story of Danish Film – Sport in Denmark – Garden Colonies in Denmark – Copenhagen, Capital of a Democracy – Aarhus, Meeting Place of Tradition and Progress – The Limfjord, its Towns and People – Funen, the Heart of Denmark

DANES OF THE PRESENT AND PAST

Danish Literature – Contemporary Danish Composers – Arne Jacobsen, by P. E. Skriver – Søren Kierkegaard, by Frithiof Brandt – N. F. S. Grundtvig, by Kaj Thaning

DANISH REFERENCE PAPERS

The Danish Mother's Aid Centres – Employers and Workers – The Ombudsman – Care of the Aged in Denmark

PERIODICALS

Contact with Denmark. Published annually in English, French, German, Italian, Netherlandish.

Musical Denmark, nos. 1–30. Published annually in English.

What can we learn from one another?

Aim and work of the Danish Institute

Det danske Selskab, The Danish Institute is an independent non-profit institution for cultural exchange between Denmark and other countries. Abroad it gives information about Danish life, thought, and work, particularly in the field of education, social welfare and other aspects of everyday existence; at home it helps spread knowledge of cultural affairs in other countries. Its work of information is thus based on the idea of mutuality and treated as a comparative study of cultural development at home and abroad by raising the question: What can we learn from one another? The work of the Danish Institute, preferably aiming at provincial regions, is done mainly in three ways:

1) By branches of the Danish Institute abroad – in Great Britain (Edinburgh), the Benelux countries (Brussels), France (Rouen), Switzerland (Zürich), Italy (Milan), West Germany (Dortmund) and its contacts in the USA and other countries. Lectures, reference work, the teaching of Danish, exhibitions, concerts, film shows, radio and television programmes as well as study tours and summer schools are an important part of the work of representatives of the Institutes that have been established abroad.

2) Summer seminars and study tours both in Denmark and abroad. Participants come from Denmark and other countries. The study tours bring foreign experts to Denmark and take Danish experts abroad. Teachers, librarians, architects and persons engaged in social welfare and local government make up a large part.

3) Publication of books and reference papers in foreign languages. Primary and Folk High Schools in Denmark, the library system, welfare services, cooperative movement, handicrafts, architecture, literature, art and music, life and work of prominent Danes are among the main subjects.

The author Martin A. Hansen called the Danish Institute a Folk High School beyond the borders: »In fact the work of the Danish Institute abroad has its roots in our finest traditions of popular education, which go right back to Grundtvig and Kold. The means and methods used are modern, the materials the very best and the approach to the work is cultural in the truest meaning af the word«.